The Natural Approach

Other Titles of Interest

The Natural Approach

Language Acquisition in the classroom

Stephen D. Krashen   •   Tracy D. Terrell

Alemany Press

Prentice Hall Regents, Englewood Cliffs, NJ 07632

© 1983 by Alemany Press
Published by Prentice-Hall Regents
A Division of Simon & Schuster
Englewood Cliffs, NJ 07632

Printed in the United States of America

10 9 8 7 6 5 4 3 2 1

ISBN   0-13-612029-6

Prentice-Hall International (UK) Limited, *London*
Prentice-Hall of Australia Pty. Limited, *Sydney*
Prentice-Hall Canada Inc., *Toronto*
Prentice-Hall Hispanoamericana, S.A., *Mexico*
Prentice-Hall of India Private Limited, *New Delhi*
Prentice-Hall of Japan, Inc., *Tokyo*
Simon & Schuster Asia Pte. Ltd., *Signapore*
Editora Prentice-Hall do Brasil, Ltda., *Rio de Janeiro*

TABLE of CONTENTS

PREFACE

This is not the first attempt to present a new approach to the teaching of second and foreign languages based on a new theory of language. Earlier attempts, most notably audiolingual approaches, have not met with great success. We think that this has happened for several reasons. A major problem was that the theories were not actually theories of language acquisition, but theories of something else; for example, the structure of language. Also, the application of the theory, the methodology, was not always adequately field-tested. What looked reasonable to the university professor on paper did not always work out in the classroom.

The Natural Approach, we hope, does not have these weaknesses. It is based on an empirically grounded theory of second language acquisition, which has been supported by a large number of scientific studies in a wide variety of language acquisition and learning contexts. In addition, it has been used by many classroom teachers in different circumstances teaching various languages and this experience has helped to shape the Approach over the last seven years.

The central hypothesis of the theory is that language acquisition occurs in only one way: by understanding messages. We acquire language when we obtain comprehensible input, when we understand what we hear or read in another language. This means that acquisition is based primarily on what we hear and understand, not what we say. The goal, then, of elementary language classes, according to this view, is to supply comprehensible input, the crucial ingredient in language acquisition, and to bring the student to the point where he or she can understand language outside the classroom. When this happens, the acquirer can utilize the real world, as well as the classroom, for progress.

The Natural Approach, then, is a way to do this. It is for beginners and is designed to help them become intermediates. We do not pretend that the Natural Approach is the only approach to language instruction which is capable of accomplishing this goal; there are other fine approaches which provide comprehensible input in a variety of innovative ways and which have been demonstrated to be effective. The Natural Approach, however, is relatively simple to use and it is easily adapted to a variety of situations (e.g. foreign language, second language, public school, adult education, bilingual programs, etc.) and can be easily modified to deal with different types of students (e.g. adults, children) with different cognitive styles. The Natural Approach, unlike some newer approaches, need not be adopted in whole; we are encouraged by instructors who have initiated Natural Approach in part within their regular programs and who report dramatic improvement in their students' abilities to use their new language for communication and in their attitudes toward language study in general.

At the time this book was written, our confidence in the Natural Approach was based primarily on underlying theory (itself supported by considerable empirical evidence) and the enthusiastic reactions of students and instructors. Since the completion of the manuscript, a direct test of the Natural Approach has been carried out. Professor Wilfried Voge, in a study reported at the International Con-

gress of Applied Linguistics in 1981, compared college level German taught
according to the Natural Approach with a "contextualized grammar" approach
(similar to the "direct method" in which all teacher-talk is in the second language, but directed towards explicit teaching of grammar). Voge reported that
Natural Approach students, after one semester, outperformed controls on tests of
speaking and writing, producing a wider range of vocabulary, transmitting more
information, more language, and greater accuracy in their syntax. On a discrete-
point grammar test, the two groups performed equally. This study suggests that
we do not necessarily sacrifice accuracy for fluency with a communicative
approach; the Natural Approach students did as well on the grammar test, even
though they studied grammar significantly less than the controls had. Their superiority in measures of communication, moreover, suggests that they have a better
chance of continuing to improve: better communication ability means more
communication and more comprehensible input outside the class.

There are many people we wish to thank for their contributions to the development of Natural Approach. Ken Fish, Spanish teacher at Corona Del Mar High
School in Newport Beach, California, was the first to "dare" to use such a
radically different approach to language instruction. Richard Barrutia, then Chair
of the Department of Spanish and Portuguese, at the University of California,
Irvine, was our first defender and allowed us to use Natural Approach on a large
scale with the students of Spanish and their graduate student instructors. Wilfried
Voge, Department of German, University of California, Irvine, and Ramón
Araluce, Department of Spanish and Portuguese, University of Southern California, Los Angeles, were the first to try to implement Natural Approach with a
large number of untrained instructors and college students. Now, of course, the
number of instructors using Natural Approach is in the hundreds and it would be
impossible to thank those who have made suggestions for improvements and
even new techniques over the years. As will be apparent, Natural Approach has
been influenced by the splendid work of James Asher (Total Physical Response),
by Ben Clay Christensen (Affective Activities), by Beverly Galyean (Confluent
Education) and by Gertrude Moscowitz (Humanistic Learning). Also, several
ESL instructors have produced materials for classroom use based on Natural
Approach principles. We will mention only a few names and hope that those
whose names are not included will not feel offended: Sandra Anderson, Irvine
Unified School District, Irvine, California, who first used Natural Approach in a
Bilingual-ESL Program, Guillermo Lopez, of the Office of Bilingual Bicultural
Education of the State of California, who included principles of Natural Approach
in the "Theoretical Framework" for Bilingual Programs in the State of California,
Merrill Swain and Michael Canale, of the Ontario Institute for Studies in Education, Toronto, for their input regarding the connection between Natural Approach
and Immersion Programs in Canada, Jeanne Egasse, Instructor of Spanish and
Linguistics, Saddleback Community College, North Campus, Irvine, California,
for her dedication to Natural Approach in the form of workshops and for "acquiring" Hebrew via Natural Approach instruction in order to demonstrate that

Natural Approach also "works" with non-Indo-European languages. We would also like to thank Judy Winn-Bell Olsen, Roger Olsen, Sharron Bassano, Philip Hauptman, and Robin Scarcella for their comments on an earlier version of the manuscript.

And we thank our students, who have shown us that normal human beings can indeed acquire another language in the classroom.

Stephen D. Krashen
Tracy D. Terrell

Chapter One

Introduction

TRADITIONAL AND NON-TRADITIONAL APPROACHES TO
LANGUAGE TEACHING

Early Viewpoints
Traditional Direct Methods
The Reading Method
The Audiolingual Method
Communicative Approaches and Methodologies

AN OVERVIEW: THEORY AND NATURAL APPROACH

Acquisition and Learning
How Acquisition Takes Place
The Natural Approach and Language Acquisition

TRADITIONAL AND NON-TRADITIONAL APPROACHES TO LANGUAGE TEACHING

The study of other languages is probably recent in terms of the history of mankind. The acquisition of other languages through using them for purposes of communication is, on the other hand, as old as language itself. Throughout his history, man has learned to use languages other than his native tongue for communicating with members of other language groups and other cultures. It is unlikely that much use was made of formal grammar studies to aid in this task since it is doubtful that such studies or even such knowledge existed. Even today with the vast amount of linguistic knowledge available about the languages of the world, it is likely that most ability to communicate in another language is acquired in what we will call "traditional" ways, i.e., through communicative practice in real situations using the language for specific functions. This is as true in the marketplace of underdeveloped regions of Africa as it is in the case of the so-called guest workers in various industrialized countries of Europe.

We will refer to this method of acquiring the ability to communicate in another language directly without instruction in its grammar as the traditional approach because the evidence seems clear that in fact this is how most people have traditionally acquired languages. Normally when we think of traditional methods of teaching and learning other languages, we think of the methods and approaches most often used in academic situations. The word "traditional" brings to mind a picture of the old schoolmaster with his dreaded ruler, ready to pounce on unwary students who make a mistake in their Latin declensions. We think of "new" methods as a revolt against these traditional and staid practices; and if tradition is to be defined in terms of American education, this is not an unjust view.

Our viewpoint, on the other hand, is that tradition in European and American education is not representative of the normal way mankind has dealt with communicating with speakers of other languages. It is, in our opinion, an aberration which may have had its roots in the period between the Renaissance and the early nineteenth century. We will examine in some detail this development since it forms the backdrop for all that is to come in this book.

Early Viewpoints

After the gradual acceptance of the modern vernacular tongues of Western Europe and with the loss of universal fluency in Latin as a medium of communication across cultures, the value of acquiring communicative competence in other languages was more acutely recognized. Although we cannot imagine that masses of illiterate peasants travelled enough to need fluency in languages other than their native tongues, it was certainly the case, then as now, that in border areas those who had need to communicate in other languages acquired the ability to do so directly from participation in these communicative experiences.

The upper classes, on the other hand, cultivated language skills usually by sending their sons or daughters to the regions in which the desired language was spoken or by bringing a native speaker to the household to allow for opportunities for natural interchange in the new tongue.

It is during the 1600's that texts aimed at aiding the learners in their progress in the new language appeared. The common underlying characteristic of these early texts is that they made little or no use of the learner's native language. Thus, they were what we would later call "direct method" texts since they advocated learning a language much in the same way we learn our first language. In fact Titone points out that even Latin, which was certainly no longer widely used for oral communication, was taught by oral methods. He mentions conversational handbooks, the famous *Diologi* or *Colloqui,* compiled by such authorities as Heyden, Cordier, Fr. Van Tomme, and so forth.[1]

Along with this long tradition of learning language in a direct fashion, i.e., by engaging in oral communication without reference to either grammar or one's native language, the study of grammar per se must have existed for many years. Both Romans and Greeks were skilled grammarians and the study of grammar was highly valued by members of the upper classes. What is not obvious is whether they used the study of grammar as a means for learning another language or simply as a goal, worthy in and of itself, after one had acquired fluency and competency in the new tongue. During the Middle Ages it is certain that much time was spent studying Latin grammar in the monasteries of Europe. However, Latin was also used as a medium of daily communication. Thus, although grammar was studied, it is not clear at all that this is the way in which competence in Latin was acquired. It is more probable that the major portion of language ability was acquired through daily use of Latin for real communicative needs; the study of grammar was considered to be more valuable in the analysis of texts and in copying.

It is clear, however, that the study of Latin grammar was highly valued and affected both the study of the grammar of one's native tongue as well as the more formalized study of other languages. Translation between Latin and the vernacular became commonplace and indeed, a knowledge of grammar was "considered an essential tool in the task of translation." In these years the use of interlinear translations became common and many saw learning another language as equatable with learning to translate from one language to another. Roger Ascham (1515-68), for example, used translation extensively in his *The Scholemaster* to teach Latin. [2]

We cannot be sure why a more formal approach to language teaching became so popular. The publication of texts which purported to teach languages based on paradigms, declensions, conjugations and rules of sentence construction multiplied extensively in this period. Mallison speculates that it was due to the fact that Latin, perhaps the language most studied by the intelligentsia and upper classes, had ceased to be a normal vehicle for daily communication. He continues:

it became a mental gymnastic, the supremely dead language, a disciplined and systematic study of which was held to be indispensable as a basis for all forms of higher education. Classical studies were then intended and made to produce an excellent mental discipline, a fortitude of spirit and a broad humane understanding of life. They succeeded triumphantly for the times in their objective. [3]

Whatever the reason, grammar-based approaches swept the western world. Titone reports that by the nineteenth century, textbook compilers "were mainly determined to codify the foreign language into frozen rules of morphology and syntax to be explained and eventually memorized. Oral work was reduced to a minimum, while a handful of written exercises, constructed at random, came as a sort of appendix of the rules." [4]

Bahlsen describes the process and method in painful detail. He described the method he used in studying French as:

> a barren waste of insipid sentence translation. Committing words to memory, translating sentences, drilling irregular verbs, later memorizing, repeating, and applying grammatical rules with their exceptions — that was and remained our main occupation, for not until the last years of the high schools with the nine-year curriculum did French reading come to anything like prominence and that was the time when free compositions of the foreign language were to be written. [5]

It is certainly not the case that such methods produced then, or for that matter have ever produced, communication skills. Fluency in spoken French for Bahlsen had to come then just as today by real experience in natural communicative situations.

According to Buchanan and MacPhee, exercises for the purposes of drill in teaching a foreign language were developed around the beginning of the eighteenth century to illustrate rules and exceptions. They comment that such sentences prepared to illustrate the rules were difficult and often absurd. [6]

So much has been written on the formal grammar-based approaches to the learning of other languages that it is not necessary to repeat this information. Any reader of this book will no doubt have experienced grammar-based language teaching since these sorts of methodologies and approaches have dominated and continue to dominate North American education to the present. We do want to point out that even in the period of domination of grammar-based approaches from, say the 1700's to the present, there were always those who accepted the importance of grammar and grammatical analyses, and still opposed grammar-based approaches, opting for more "natural" or "direct" approaches. [7]

Traditional Direct Methods

The reaction to grammar-based approaches and the subsequent call to use more traditional ways of learning other languages came from diverse sources and in different ways with various labels. The approaches have been called natural, psychological, phonetic, new, reform, direct, analytic, imitative and so forth.

What they have in common is that they refer to traditional ways of learning based on the use of language in communicative situations usually without recourse to the native language.[8]

The first trend to establish itself with a name was the **natural method.** The report of the Committee of Twelve in 1901 originated by the Modern Language Association describes it as follows:

> In its extreme form the method consisted of a series of monologues by the teacher interspersed with exchanges of question and answer between the instructor and the pupil — all in the foreign language... A great deal of pantomime accompanied the talk. With the aid of this gesticulation, by attentive listening, and by dint of much repetition the learner came to associate certain acts and objects with certain combinations of the sounds and finally reached the point of reproducing the foreign words of phrases... Not until a considerable familiarity with the spoken word was attained was the scholar allowed to see the foreign language in print. The study of grammar was reserved for a still later period. [9]

The so-called **psychological method** was similar. Its basic characteristic was that the instructor attempted to make the association of ideas either with each other or with something concrete. Frequently used were objects, diagrams, charts and "pantomime was a frequent device." [10]

The **series method** advocated by François Gouin was perhaps the best known technique used by the psychological methodologists. The technique is simple: it consists of relating activities in a series relating to a specific activity. For example, if we wished to talk about washing the car we could describe the sequence with a series of statements such as: *First we get a bucket, then we fill it with water and soap. We must have either a sponge or a rag. We use the soap and water to scrub the entire car,* etc.

Gouin developed this technique after a long struggle trying to learn to speak and understand German through formal grammar-based methods. If these methods could have produced communicative competence, they should have with Gouin since he had been trained in languages and language study. However, their total failure and his turning to observations of how children learn a second language is one of the most impressive personal testimonials in the recorded annals of language learning. [11]

The **phonetic method** belongs also in this group because of its insistence on oral expression. It is mostly associated with the name of Vietor in Germany but was popular with practitioners of the newly developed phonetic science. The students were drilled first in the discrimination and production of the sounds of the new language using short idiomatic phrases and making liberal use of phonetic symbols. The normal script was not used at first. These phrases were turned into dialogs and stories. All grammar was studied inductively, that is, students had to discover rules through a problem-solving approach, rather than being told what they were. (This was true of all of the methods in this group). [12]

These traditional ideas had the most effect on language teaching in France.

The term **méthode directe** refers to the teaching of languages without resorting to translation and without using the native language. The term originated from a publication of the French Minister of Public Instruction in 1901.[13]

The **direct method** was also very popular in certain circles in the United States at the beginning of the 20th century. The professional literature in this period is full of debates between grammar method adherents and direct method followers.[14] It is, with minor modification, the method preferred by academies and specialized schools whose sole purpose is to train persons in skills in another language. The Berlitz Schools are the most famous, but also the various foreign language schools such as the Alliance Française and the Goethe Institute, sponsored by the French and German governments respectively, have strongly adhered to such methods. We suspect this is because such institutions cannot, by their very existence, tolerate failure — their students must learn to communicate or they will have no students. The massive failure of public school instruction can be lamented, but it is, in a sense, tolerable since the students are a captive audience.

This is not to say that the direct method was not applied in public institutions. Since the turn of the century up to the present day, there have always been those individuals who have adhered more or less to direct method techniques. This seems to have especially been true with French classes as opposed to German and Spanish instruction, which for the most part seem to have remained tied to grammar-based methodologies.

The Reading Method

There was one early attempt at reforming and unifying language methodology early this century. This attempt was derived from a study of foreign language methodology and an extensive poll of the foreign language profession on generally accepted goals for language study in the United States. The study was published as the Modern Foreign Language Study and was produced by a committee under the direction of Algernon Coleman and sponsored by the Carnegie Corporation. The most important single volume produced by the study was Coleman's *The Teaching of Modern Foreign Languages in the United States.* This report found that of the generally recognized four skills — listening comprehension, speaking, reading, and writing — only the reading skill was acceptable as the primary goal to all of the members of the profession. Consequently the Committee looked at the relevant research to determine what methods would produce students with reading skills in the standard two-year secondary school sequence. The report stated that:

> experience and statistical evidence in teaching the vernacular indicate that the amount of reading that the pupils do is directly related to achievement both in rate of silent reading and in comprehension. Furthermore, experiments show conclusively that increasing the amount of reading that is required results in rapid progress in rate and comprehension.

Thus, the report recommended that the amount of reading in foreign language classes be drastically increased. [15]

One cannot simply increase the amount of reading, however, without con-comitant changes in how the reading is done. At the time this report was issued, it would be safe to say that most classes were taught using a grammar-based method with heavy emphasis on translation as a goal. Other classes using direct methods would have emphasized oral skills with little emphasis on reading, and, of course, none on translation. When recommending an increase in the amount of reading, the committee specifically defined reading:

> They will practice reading silently, both in and out of class, endeavoring delib-erately to understand complete sentences and longer passages without trans-lation into English. [16]

Thus, the report opted for extensive reading, i.e., reading for content rather than intensive reading, i.e., detailed grammatical analysis of smaller passages. All ac-tivities in the class were to converge on developing extensive reading. In the two-year course the student was to have read (for content only) almost 1000 pages of foreign language text.

The details of the method are not of interest here. The emphasis on exten-sive reading and the rejection of translation was, however, a return to "tradi-tional" approaches, although the focus on a single skill as the goal of foreign language study would seem rather extreme today. We must remember, however, that opportunities for the average American student to travel to Europe to use French or German or to South America or Mexico to use Spanish were very few compared to the opportunities of students today.

The report was influential in increasing interest in graded readers which used frequency counts for selection of both vocabulary and structure. In order to train the student to read extensively, the material needed to be at the correct level. Although these abridgements of classic works of literature based on fre-quency counts later fell out of fashion, most are still available and useful for the language student, as we shall see in later sections of this book.

The report did not really have the desired impact on instruction. Those who strongly disagreed with the Committee in terms of goals for language instruc-tion continued to emphasize the oral skills or the grammar skills they deemed most important. Especially those trained in translation methods attempted to increase the amount of translation to the further detriment of oral skills. It is pretty safe to say that by the period of World War II and its aftermath, the language profession in the United States had settled back into formal grammar-based methods which stressed conscious knowledge of grammar rules and ability to do sight translations. Traditional direct methods survived only sporad-ically in places in which individuals had developed especially good programs. One particularly famous example is De Sauzé's Cleveland Plan. [17] This plan has been described (Titone, 1968:81) as a "multiple integrated approach, in which all the four basic skills are taught simultaneously on the basis of the students' real life experiences." [18]

The Audiolingual Method

What did have a significant impact was the Second World War. The impact was felt from two directions. First, the public became painfully aware of the failure of the language teaching profession to train students in communicative abilities. The soldiers and others who found themselves in foreign language areas were unprepared to deal with simple communication; the public wanted to know why. The answer is of course simple: methods in which students never engage in real communication cannot be expected to produce students able to communicate using the language they study.

The other source of influence which was to have a profound effect was the United States Army language programs. With the advent of World War II the military complex of the United States suddenly found itself in need of personnel trained in a large number and wide variety of languages. They had a special need for persons who could learn languages of certain indigenous groups of southeast Asia and the islands of the Pacific, some of whose languages had not yet been studied or even codified in written form. They turned to the only group of persons who could have provided this sort of expertise: the American descriptive linguists who had worked extensively with American Indian languages. These linguists were called on to organize language classes, write materials and in general provide expertise in these areas. The schools were informally reported to be a great success: students learned to communicate in a wide variety of languages and the goals of the military with regard to language training were met.

Since these courses were apparently so successful, it is worth our time to look at least briefly at the components of an Army language course during this period. It consisted typically of two sessions — one in which situational-based dialogs were practiced and memorized, followed by oral drills consisting of sentences illustrating the major syntactic patterns and form classes of the language. These drill sessions were conducted either by a linguist familiar with the language or by a native speaker trained by a linguist. The dialog-drill sessions were then followed by conversation sessions with a native speaker; these were usually constructed around real life situations, often those of the dialogs. The classes were small, usually under 10 persons, allowing for ample opportunity to engage in communication experiences.

In retrospect, it was probably due to these intensive communicative sessions that these courses were so successful. This is somewhat ironic, since these communication sessions were not to be included in the Audiolingual Method which would be derived, for the most part, from the techniques used in the "drill" sessions.

The success of these classes added to the general public's recognition of the failure of the language teaching profession. For example, a survey of secondary enrollments showed that in 1949 and 1955 only about 14% of the secondary population enrolled in language courses and as late as 1957, 56% of the secondary schools in the United States offered no foreign language courses. [19]

The Soviet Union's launching of Sputnik, the first earth satellite, in 1957, was beneficial; by 1958 the Congress of the United States had passed the National Defense Education Act in which the study of modern foreign languages was defined and seen as an important goal in the security and defense of the United States. The next 10 years provided the setting for intense activity in the development of methods and materials for language instruction using the Army methods as a partial model. This new methodology came to be known as **audiolingualism** because of its emphasis on the teaching of oral skills (listening and speaking) before reading and writing. [20]

Audiolingualism swept the country in a wave of reaction against the grammar-translation method. This far-reaching reform was supported by the linguistic establishment and in part by a theory of psychology known as behaviorism. It was supported by the U.S. government by various grants and contracts and by the national language teachers' groups such as the Modern Language Association. [21]

It is perhaps unfair to audiolingualism to present its tenets in a few short paragraphs. It is not, however, our purpose to write a history of methodology, but to place the Natural Approach in its historic context. We assume that our readers are familiar with audiolingualism, since it continues to influence teaching methodology in many parts of North America and the original audiolingual materials (and their successors) are still used in a great many places. [22]

The basic tenet of audiolingual methodology is that language performance consists of a set of habits in the use of language structures and patterns. Students were not necessarily expected to understand grammar and grammar rules; indeed rules were to serve more as summaries of established behavior. To achieve the goals, the classroom activities were to consist of (1) new material, both lexical and grammatical, presented in the form of dialogs which were to represent pieces of real communication, (2) a series of pattern drills in which the structures and vocabulary introduced in the dialog would be manipulated until the structures became unconscious habits for the student, and (3) recombination response material in which the student tried to apply the newly acquired structure in guided semi-free conversations. Presumably the student would, at some point after an unspecified length of study, arrive at the stage at which the structures and phonological system had been established as habits and could focus on the message, allowing for real communication in the target language.

Audiolingual practices have in recent years come under strong criticism from theoretical linguists, most of whom now are working with a different theoretical model than when audiolingualism was first developed, psychologists who have tended to reject the behaviorist models in favor of cognitive models of learning, and most importantly from teachers and students who found the specific practices excruciatingly boring. [23]

While there were serious problems with audiolingual practices, the defects of the approach have been also exaggerated by its opponents. One of the first problems to be corrected was the insistence on the development of oral skills with no use of printed materials. There were two reasons for this principle: children learn the oral skills without reference to written material, and the written code of the native language will supposedly cause interference in learning the target language, resulting in the transfer of native language habits of pronunciation into the target language. In addition, many had experienced the total dependence on the written word of the grammar-based methods which preceded audiolingualism. Most felt strongly that this dependence had to be broken. In all three cases, the observations were accurate: children do not use the printed word for initial language acquisition, the transfer of pronunciation features from the native language may occur when the student sees the printed word in the target language, and students in grammar-based approaches generally became completely reading-dependent. However, the cure, which was to present all material, both dialogs and drills, without permitting students to see how the sounds were written, was a disaster. It normally took three or four times as long to teach the material without the aid of orthography. Students invented their own systems of writing to record what they were to memorize and the entire experience was frustrating for both students and teachers alike. In addition, once the students finally were allowed to see written what they had been learning, transfer of the pronunciation errors might occur in any case. Certainly an improvement in pronunciation did not compensate for the morale problems created by denying access to the printed word.

There were several other criticisms of audiolingualism. One was the fact that habit formation simply did not happen at such a fast rate; real habits (subconscious language acquisition, see Chapter Two) take much longer to establish than is possible with any series of drills. Still another problem had to do with the rule summaries. As mentioned above, the statement of rules at the end of each lesson was intended to serve as a descriptive summary of the behavior already established. Nevertheless, in actual practice they often served as the basis of inductive learning, the material presented in the dialog and pattern drill leading the student to the correct conscious mental representation of the target structure. As several scholars have pointed out, inductive learning is not suited to all students. [24] The reaction to this problem was to return to deductive learning, with the instructor first explaining the rule and then the students practicing the rule using drills of various sorts. The only substantial difference between these practices and the grammar-translation methods which preceded them was that in this modified form of audiolingualism, practice was primarily oral, rather than written.

Still another criticism of audiolingualism was that students simply repeated the drills without understanding what they were saying, being focused neither on the meaning of the sentence nor on the new rules they contained. As we shall see later (Chapter Two), there is an even more serious criticism that can be made: even if the message or rule involved is understood and paid attention to, such drills are not real communication since they transmit no real message.

The **cognitive** movement was a return to grammar explanation followed by various sorts of exercises to practice the rule in question. [25] These exercises could be of the type used by previous grammar-translation methods or audio-lingual, but in both cases, the emphasis was on conscious understanding of the rule being practiced. Chastain states that the "purpose of a cognitive exercise is the comprehension of forms, the conscious learning of forms, and the conscious selection of forms to fit the context." [26]

Thus, cognitivism in language teaching is simply a return to grammar-based instruction practically identical to the earlier methods which have dominated American public education since its inception and which have been an unqualified failure in producing students with communicative competence in the language they are studying. The main difference is the addition of a "communication practice" component in the cognitive approach. The Pennsylvania Project, the most extensive study to compare audiolingual methods with cognitive based methodologies showed that after two years of study there were no differences in student performances in any of the skills except reading. Most interestingly student opinion of foreign language instruction declined throughout instruction regardless of the two methods involved. [27]

Communicative Approaches and Methodologies

It is almost a paradox that what man seems perfectly equipped to do when the the need and opportunity arise — acquire the ability to communicate in another language — seems so elusive to language classes and instructors in North American education. We believe that one of the primary reasons is that educators have been misled by innovations and shortcuts. What we have referred to as the traditional point of view is, from all available evidence, still correct: to acquire the ability to communicate in another language, one must use that language in a communicative situation. Communicative ability is usually acquired quite rapidly; grammatical accuracy, on the other hand, increases only slowly and after much experience using the language. The mistake the innovators have made is to assume that a conscious understanding of grammar is a prerequisite to acquiring communicative competence. That such an understanding might be helpful in some situations for some students is not in question — that it is a prerequisite for all students is patently false. Thus, any grammar-based method which purports to develop communication skills will fail with the majority of students. Only a few will be able to work their way through a grammar course, be it grammar-translation, audiolingual, or cognitive, and persevere long enough finally to put themselves in communicative situations and acquire the competence they have been striving for. This usually happens in the American educational system in the third or fourth years of language study or often even later. What is clear, is that most students never make it through this ordeal.

There are several methods which have been developed recently which are based on traditional principles of language acquisition. The central principle of each is that to acquire communicative competence the key component of the course must be to allow the student to use the language for real communication and that exercise and drill are neither necessary nor sufficient. Newmark and Reibel stated this principle.

> Systematic organization of the grammatical form of the language material exposed to the learner is neither necessary nor sufficient for his mastery of the language...Presentation of particular instances of language in contexts which exemplify their meaning and use is both sufficient and necessary... Systematic teaching of structure (as in structure drills) imposes formal rather than useful organization of language material. To plan teaching programs on the basis of formal properties of sentences is thus incompatible with the only necessary and sufficient method known for learning a language. [28]

Among the communicative approaches we are familiar with are Asher's Total Physical Response, Lozanov's Suggestopedia and Curran's Community Language Learning. While several of these methods include formal grammar study, all are communication-based, and if the reports in the professional literature and preliminary reports from colleagues are to be believed, all produce far superior results to grammar-based approaches.

The approach we will present in this book is in many ways the natural, direct method rediscovered. It is similar to other communicative approaches being developed today. We find ourselves in almost complete agreement with methodologists of other centuries and with methodologists today using diverse techniques. What we do claim for the new Natural Approach is that (1) the latest research in first and second language acquisition supports its tenets very strongly, and (2) it is adaptable to many teaching contexts for students of all ages. Unfortunately this is not the case with some of the more specialized communicative approaches such as Suggestopedia which require special equipment and very extensive teacher training. In addition, whereas some of the other approaches seem to be based on one or two central techniques (Suggestopedia, Total Physical Response, Silent Way, Counseling-Learning), the Natural Approach is highly flexible with regard to the sorts of teaching techniques used in the classroom and is able to incorporate any of the techniques of these approaches where appropriate, without depending exclusively on any of them.

We have written this book with two purposes in mind. First, it serves as an introduction to the Monitor Theory of language acquisition and learning; the hypotheses of the Monitor Theory form the base of the tenets which underlie the Natural Approach. Second, it will serve as a handbook for instructors who wish to use a communication-based approach in the classroom. Even if the Natural Approach is not adopted in whole, we feel that any reduction of the dominance of grammar-based methods will improve language teaching.[30] All human beings can acquire additional languages, but they must have the desire or the need to acquire the language and the opportunity to use the language they study for real communicative purposes.

AN OVERVIEW:
THEORY AND NATURAL APPROACH

In this section we provide a brief description of the Natural Approach preceded by a summary of the theory of second language acquisition that supports it. More detailed treatment of theory is contained in Chapter Two, while Chapters Three through Seven contain more specific information about how the approach works in practice.

We hope it will become clear to the reader that it is difficult and undesirable to present methodological principles of the Natural Approach without some reference to theoretical concepts. We keep the discussion of theory in this chapter to a minimum however, and present only some of the central findings in language acquisition research that are helpful in understanding the Natural Approach. These findings are presented without argumentation, without supporting data for now, to allow the reader to get a global picture of the theory easily and quickly.

Acquisition and Learning

The most important and useful theoretical point is the **acquisition-learning** distinction, the hypothesis that adult language students have two distinct ways of developing skills and knowledge in a second language. Simply, **acquiring** a language is "picking it up," i.e., developing ability in a language by using it in natural, communicative situations. Children acquire their first language, and most probably, second languages as well. As we shall see in Chapter Two, adults also can acquire: they do not usually do it quite as well as children, but it appears that language acquisition is the central, most important means for gaining linguistic skills even for an adult.

Language **learning** is different from acquisition. Language learning is "knowing the rules," having a conscious knowledge about grammar. According to recent research, it appears that formal language learning is not nearly as important in developing communicative ability in second languages as previously thought. Many researchers now believe that language acquisition is responsible for the ability to understand and speak second languages easily and well. Language learning may only be useful as an editor, which we will call a **Monitor.** We use acquisition when we initiate sentences in second languages, and bring in learning only as a kind of after-thought to make alterations and corrections.

Conscious rules have therefore a limited function in second language use; we refer to conscious grammar rules only to make changes, hopefully corrections. These changes can come before the sentence is actually spoken or written, or they can come after (self-correction). The function of conscious learning seems even more limited when we consider that in order to monitor our speech successfully, that is, in order to make corrections, several conditions have to be met: (1) the second language user has to have **time** to inspect the utterance before it is spoken, (2) the speaker has to be consciously concerned about **correctness,** and (3) he has to **know** the rule. In natural conversation, all of these conditions are rarely met. Normal conversation tends to be quite rapid, and the speaker's attention is usually on **what** is being said, not **how** it is being said. In addition, our conscious knowledge of grammar covers only a small portion of the rules of a language. On the other hand, all three conditions are met quite well on grammar tests. These are usually written rather than oral and are designed to make students think about language form and not the message: they usually focus almost exclusively on rules that have just been taught in the classroom. In this situation knowledge which has been learned is, of course, of great help.

Knowledge of conscious rules can be helpful in situations other than formal grammar exams. In writing and in prepared speech, performers do have time to apply conscious knowledge of the second language and can use this knowledge to improve the form of their output by monitoring. Ideally, learning will supplement acquired competence in such cases, performers using learning to supply aspects of language that have not yet been acquired. Such items may not add much to the communicative value of the output, but they may give a more polished, a more "educated" look. In writing, learning may also be useful for some spelling and punctuation problems.

Difficulties arise when performers, especially beginners, become over-concerned with correctness in communicative situations, trying to check their output against conscious rules at all times. This overuse of the Monitor results in hesitancy and subsequent difficulty in participating in conversation. Ideal or optimal use of the Monitor occurs when second language speakers use the rules they have learned without interfering with communication.

How Acquisition Takes Place

We already know a great deal about encouraging language learning. Indeed learning occupies the central position in language classes in all grammar-based approaches. If acquisition is more important than learning for developing communicative ability as the evidence suggests, we need to concern ourselves with the question of how people acquire. According to research in second language acquisition, it is thought that acquisition can take place only when people **understand** messages in the target language. Incomprehensible input (e.g. listening to an unknown language on the radio) does not seem to help language acquisition. We acquire when we focus on what is being said, rather than how it is said. We acquire when language is used for communicating real ideas.

While comprehensible input is necessary for acquisition, it is not sufficient. There are **affective** prerequisites to acquisition, as every teacher and language student knows. Briefly, the acquirer has to be "open" to the input in order to fully utilize it for acquisition. According to research, factors that contribute to a *low affective filter* include positive orientation to speakers of the language, acquiring in a low anxiety situation, and at least some degree of acquirer self-confidence.

Spoken fluency in second languages is not taught directly. Rather, the ability to speak fluently and easily in a second language **emerges** by itself, after a sufficient amount of competence has been acquired through input. It may take some time before any real spoken fluency develops. With many acquirers there is a **silent period** which may last from a few hours to several months, depending on the situation and the age of the acquirer. Initial production is typically not very accurate. Very early speech is quite flawed, with acquirers using mostly simple words and short phrases. It also contains few function words or grammatical markers. Gradually more complex constructions are acquired (as the acquirer obtains more comprehensible input) and the grammatical markers are "filled in."

The Natural Approach and Language Acquisition

The first principle of the Natural Approach is that **comprehension precedes production,** i.e., listening (or reading) comprehension precedes speaking (or writing) abilities. This follows from the hypotheses presented earlier that acquisition is the basis for production ability and that in order for acquisition to take place, the acquirer must understand messages. Thus, the starting point in language instruction is to help acquirers understand what is being said to them. (This is, of course, also the case for acquirers not in classroom situations.) Some of the implications of this principle are that (1) the instructor always uses the target language, (2) the focus of the communication will be on a topic of interest for the student, (3) the instructor will strive at all times to help the student understand.

The second general principle of the Natural Approach is that **production** is allowed to emerge **in stages.** These stages typically consist of: (1) response by nonverbal communication, (2) response with a single word: *yes, no, there, O.K., you, me, house, run, come, on,* etc., (3) combinations of two or three words: *paper on table, me no go, where book, don't go,* etc., (4) phrases: *I want to stay. Where you going? The boy running,* etc. (5) sentences, and finally (6) more complex discourse. Grammatical accuracy is very low in early stages and increases slowly with increased opportunities for communicative interaction and acquisition. For this reason in the Natural Approach **the students are not forced to speak before they are ready.** In addition, **speech errors which do not interfere with communication are not corrected;** while the correction of errors may help learning, acquired competence comes from comprehensible input.

The third general principle of the Natural Approach is that the course **syllabus consists of communicative goals.** This means that the focus of each classroom activity is organized by topic, not grammatical structure. Thus, a possible goal may be to learn to communicate about trips the students have taken or to be able to order a meal in a restaurant. Practice of specific grammatical structures is not focused on in these activities. Our claim is that grammar will be effectively acquired if goals are communicative. Ironically, if goals are grammatical, some grammar will be learned and very little acquired. Thus, even though we are very interested in producing students who can speak with correct grammar, communicative ability and not grammatical accuracy is emphasized in beginning comprehension and production stages.

The final principle is that the activities done in the classroom aimed at acquisition must foster **a lowering of the affective filter of the students.** Activities in the classroom focus at all times on topics which are interesting and relevant to the students and encourage them to express their ideas, opinions, desires, emotions and feelings. An environment which is conducive to acquisition must be created by the instructor — low anxiety level, good rapport with the teacher, friendly relationship with other students; otherwise acquisition will be impossible. Such an atmosphere is not a luxury but a necessity.

Social differences

Notes

1. Titone 1968, p. 10.
2. Ibid., p. 10.
3. Mallison 1957, p. 8.
4. Titone 1968, p. 27.
5. Bahlsen 1905, p. 10.
6. Buchanan and MacPhee 1928, pp. 7–8.
7. Gouin 1880, [English translation is Swan, H. and Betis, V. 1892] and Palmer 1917, 1921 are notable examples.
8. Cole 1931, pp. 55–62.
9. Ibid., p. 58.
10. Ibid., p. 59.
11. For a more detailed overview of traditional "direct" methods, including an account of Gouin's contributions, see Diller 1971.
12. Cole 1931, p. 59.
13. Ibid., p. 60.
14. See for example Sparkman 1926, Williams 1923 and Donaldson 1922.
15. Titone 1968, pp. 82–4, Cole 1931, pp. 73–112 and Coleman 1929, p. 170.
16. Coleman 1929, p. 170.
17. De Sauze 1929 and McClain 1945.
18. Titone 1968, p. 81.
19. Oliva 1969, p. 5.
20. The two handbooks which best describe the theory and practice of audiolingualism are Brooks 1964 and Lado 1964.
21. The most famous sets of materials produced were audiolingual materials (A-LM) for secondary schools (Thompson, et al., 1957), and Modern Spanish (Bolinger, et al., 1960) for the university level.
22. However, the latest editions of the A-LM series (third edition) are completely new and retain very little that could correctly be considered to be audiolingual as this approach was first developed.
23. The adherents of generative-transformational theories in linguistics were especially critical of the linguists who had participated in the development of the audiolingual methodology and who, for the most part, were adherents of structuralist (descriptivist) theories of linguistics. See Chastain 1976, particularly Chapters Five and Six, for an excellent account of the theoretical differences between the two groups.
24. See for example Rivers 1964. This book was especially important in pointing out both theoretical and practical shortcomings of the audiolingual approach.
25. See, for example, papers in Lugton and Heinle 1971.
26. Chastain 1976, p. 151.
27. Ibid., pp. 158-9.
28. This important article was reprinted in Lester 1970.
29. For Asher's approach see Asher 1977. (Also Romijn and Seely 1979 and Swan 1981.) For an introduction to Lozanov's system, see Bancroft 1978, and Lozanov 1979. Curran's ideas can be found in Curran 1976, Stevick 1973 and LaForge 1971. See also Stevick 1976 and 1980 for an excellent discussion of innovative approaches including some of these.
30. In addition we believe that the Natural Approach can help to dispel the myth that English speakers cannot learn other languages.

Chapter Two

Second Language Acquisition Theory

THE THEORETICAL MODEL: FIVE HYPOTHESES

    The Acquisition-Learning Hypothesis
    The Natural Order Hypothesis
    The Monitor Hypothesis
    The Input Hypothesis
    Aspects of Second Language Acquisition Related to
      the Input Hypothesis
    The Affective Filter Hypothesis

FACTORS WHICH INFLUENCE SECOND
LANGUAGE ACQUISITION

    Second Language Aptitude
    The Role of the First Language
    Routines and Patterns
    Individual Variation
    Age Differences

The aim of this chapter is to acquaint the reader with the current state of research and theory in adult second and foreign language acquisition. We will briefly review what researchers have hypothesized about how second languages are acquired and learned on the basis of experimentation and observation. Most of the work we will report here has been done over the last ten years, and therefore is fully available only in professional journals and in technical books.

Before proceeding to list the hypotheses that summarize current work in second language acquisition, a few words of explanation are in order. First, the hypotheses are hypotheses, or guesses as to how language acquisition works. Further research may change them or even force us to reject one or more of them. In stating this warning, we are only informing the reader that language acquisition research follows the generally accepted rules of science: we make hypotheses based on existing data, and make further observations in an attempt to find supporting evidence and/or contradictory evidence. Finding supporting evidence does not prove the hypothesis: the skeptic can always ask for more evidence, but contradictory evidence can disprove our hypotheses. One good counter-example may be enough to destroy a hypothesis or a theory built on that hypothesis. So we are presenting our best guesses to date, not necessarily the ultimate truth about second language acquisition. Before the reader becomes too discouraged, however, let us assure you that the hypotheses presented here are well supported by empirical data and are thusfar unblemished by damaging counter-examples.

In this chapter we will present the set of hypotheses that make up current second language acquisition theory. In Chapter Three we will show how this theory is applied in terms of the Natural Approach and how the methodology of the Natural Approach follows from that research. We will show, in other words, how "theory" can be an extremely practical undertaking.

A final point before proceeding is that the reader will notice that the hypotheses overlap: evidence for one hypothesis may also "count" as evidence for one or more other hypotheses, and several hypotheses will be seen to be clearly interrelated. We regard this as a strength of the individual hypotheses and evidence that together, they form a coherent theory, a coherent picture of how second language competence is acquired and used in performance by adults.

THE THEORETICAL MODEL: FIVE HYPOTHESES

The Acquisition-Learning Hypothesis

This hypothesis claims that adults have two distinct ways of developing competence in second languages. The first way is via language **acquisition,** that is, by using language for real communication. Language acquisition is the "natural" way to develop linguistic ability, and is a subconscious process; children for example are not necessarily aware that they are acquiring language, they are only aware that they are communicating.

The results of language acquisition, acquired linguistic competence, are also subconscious. We are not generally "aware" of the rules of languages we have acquired. Instead, we have a "feel" for correctness: when we hear an error we may not know exactly what rule was violated, but somehow "know" that an error was committed.

The second way to develop competence in a second language is by language **learning.** Language learning is "knowing about" language, or "formal knowledge" of a language. While acquisition is subconscious, learning is conscious. Learning refers to "explicit" knowledge of rules, being aware of them and being able to talk about them. This kind of knowledge is quite different from language acquisition, which could be termed "implicit."

The Acquisition-Learning Hypothesis claims that adults can still acquire second languages, that the ability to "pick up" languages does not disappear at puberty, as some have claimed, but is still with us as adults. The Acquisition-Learning Hypothesis does not imply necessarily that adults can acquire perfectly or that they can always achieve a native level of performance in second languages. It also does not specify what aspects of language are acquired and what are learned, or how the adult performer uses acquisition and learning in performance. It only states that the processes are different and that both exist in the adult. Other hypotheses will discuss just how much adults can acquire, what parts of language are acquired, and how acquisition and learning interrelate in second language performance.

Language teaching has quite different effects on acquisition and on learning. If we examine language teaching in grammar-based approaches which emphasize explanations of rules and correction of errors, it appears that teaching is directed totally at learning and not acquisition.[1] In fact, conscious language learning is thought to be helped a great deal by teaching: its goal is the learning of conscious rules, and error correction is thought to help the learner arrive at the "right" form of the rule. If for example, a student of

English says *I goes to school every day,* and is corrected and forced to repeat the utterance correctly, the student is supposed to alter his mental vision of the third person singular rule and realize that the -s ending only goes with the third person and not the first person. [2]

Research in child language acquisition suggests quite strongly that teaching, as defined above, does not facilitate acquisition. Error correction in particular does not seem to help. Brown and his colleagues [3] have found that parents actually correct only a small portion of the child's language, for example, occasional pronunciation problems, certain verbs, and dirty words! They conclude from their research that parents attend far more to the truth value of what the child is saying rather than to the form. For example, Brown reports that a sentence such as *Her curl my hair* was not corrected by a parent in one of his studies since its meaning was clear in the context, while *Walt Disney comes on television on Tuesdays* was corrected since Walt Disney actually was on television on Wednesdays.

Despite our conclusion that language teaching is directed at learning and not acquisition, we think that it is possible to encourage acquisition very effectively in the classroom. A large part of this book will be devoted precisely to this proposition.

The acquisition-learning distinction is not new with us. Several other scholars found it useful to posit a difference between "implicit" and "explicit" learning, between mechanisms that guide "automatic" performance and mechanisms that guide "puzzle-and-problem-solving performance". [4] There is impressive evidence for the reality of the distinction, and this hypothesis plays a central role in the general theory of second language acquisition we are presenting here. Much of this evidence will be presented as we discuss the subsequent hypotheses; other evidence can be found in the technical reports and papers given in the bibliography.

Table One summarizes the characteristics of acquisition and learning.

TABLE ONE
The Acquisition-Learning Distinction

acquisition	*learning*
similar to child first language acquisition	formal knowledge of language
"picking up" a language	"knowing about" a language
subconscious	conscious
implicit knowledge	explicit knowledge
formal teaching does not help	formal teaching helps

The Natural Order Hypothesis

This hypothesis states that grammatical structures are acquired (not necessarily learned) in a predictable order. It states that we will see similarities across acquirers; certain structures will tend to be acquired early, while others will tend to be acquired late. Before giving some examples from the language acquisition research, it may be helpful to make some qualifying statements. The **Natural Order Hypothesis** does not state that every acquirer will acquire grammatical structures in the exact same order. It states rather that, in general, certain structures tend to be acquired early and to be acquired late. It also allows the possibility that structures may be acquired in groups, several at about the same time. Some examples might help to make this clear.

One of the best studied parts of grammar in language acquisition is English morphology. It is a well-established finding that there exists a natural order for the acquisition of English morphology for children acquiring English as a first language. Brown discovered that children tend to acquire certain grammatical morphemes, or "function words", relatively early, and certain others relatively late. For example, the progressive tense marker -ing, as in *He is going to work* and the plural -s, as in *two hats,* are usually among the first morphemes acquired by children. Typically late acquired are the third person singular morpheme -s, *He goes to work every day at nine,* and the *'s* possessive marker, *It is John's hat.* The "late" morphemes might come a full year after the early ones.

To illustrate the points made above about individual variation and the possibility that some morphemes come in "groups", we would not be surprised to see one child acquire -ing a bit before the plural marker, and another to acquire these two in the opposite order. A third might acquire both at about the same time. But we would be very surprised to see a child acquire a third person singular or possessive morpheme before -ing or plural.

The Natural Order Hypothesis has been confirmed for a variety of structures in child first language acquisition. Brown charted the growth of fourteen grammatical morphemes over time in three children (a longitudinal study) and found striking similarities in order of acquisition (but not in rate of acquisition, a topic we will discuss later). Brown also concluded that his results were consistent with other researchers' results. Brown's associates, Jill and Peter de Villiers, confirmed that the same similarities hold when children are studied cross-sectionally, that is, the difficulty order is similar to the acquisition order. In their study, they confirmed that those items children tend to get right more often were the same structures that Brown found were acquired early in his longitudinal research. [5]

An extremely important subsequent discovery was that children acquiring English as a second language also show a natural order for grammatical morphemes. In a series of studies, Dulay and Burt reported that children acquiring English as a second language in different parts of the United States and with different first languages (Chinese and Spanish), showed a remarkably similar difficulty order for various function words and grammatical morphemes. This result has been confirmed by most other studies using child second language acquirers. [6]

Even more astounding, in our opinion, was the finding that adults also show a natural order of grammatical morphemes. Several studies, beginning with the 1974 study by Bailey, Madden, and Krashen, show for adults what Dulay and Burt showed for children: subjects who speak different first languages show remarkably similar difficulty orders. This is important evidence for both the Natural Order Hypothesis, and as we shall see below, for the Acquisition-Learning Hypothesis. The order of acquisition for second language is not exactly the same as the order of acquisition for first language but there are some clear similarities. Table Two presents an "average" order of child and adult second language acquisition, and shows just how the first language order differs. This average order is the result of a comparison of many empirical research studies of grammatical morpheme acquisition. [7]

TABLE TWO
Average Order of Acquisition of Grammatical Morphemes for English as a Second Language (Children and Adults)

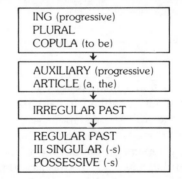

NOTES: 1. This order is derived from an analysis of empirical studies of second language acquisition in a 1981 study by Krashen. Most studies show significant correlations with the average order.

2. No claims are made about ordering relations for morphemes in the same box.

3. Many of the relationships posited here also hold for child first language acquisition, but some do not. In general, the *bound* morphemes have the same relative order for first and second language acquisition (-ing, Plural, Ir. Past, Reg. Past, III Singular, and Possessive) while Copula and Auxiliary tend to be acquired relatively later in first language acquisition than in second language acquisition.

This natural order for adult subjects seems to appear only under certain conditions. It may not appear when we give adults grammar tests, but appears reliably when we focus adults on communication. This is an important point, and it also forms the basis for our next hypothesis, the Monitor hypothesis.

We have restricted our discussion to grammatical morphemes here, since our goal was merely to illustrate the natural order hypothesis with a concrete example. There has been research in other domains of grammar. [8]

The Monitor Hypothesis

This hypothesis states that conscious learning has an extremely limited function in adult second language performance: it can only be used as a **Monitor,** or an editor. The hypothesis says that when we produce utterances in a second language, the utterance is "initiated" by the acquired system, and our conscious learning only comes into play later. We can thus use the Monitor to make changes in our utterances only after the utterance has been generated by the acquired system. This may happen before we actually speak or write, or it may happen after. When it happens after the utterance has been produced (uttered or written), it is called self-repair. Figure One represents the Monitor Model for adult second language performance.

FIGURE ONE
A Model of Adult Second Language Performance

Our fluency in production is thus hypothesized to come from what we have "picked up", what we have acquired, in natural communicative situations. Our "formal knowledge" of a second language, the rules we learned in class and from texts, is not responsible for fluency, but only has the function of checking and making repairs on the output of the acquired system.

Not only does learning have only the Monitor function, but research has also revealed that Monitor use itself is very limited. There seem to be three requirements that must be satisfied in order to use the Monitor successfully:

1. The performer has to have enough time. In rapid conversation, taking time to think about rules, such as the subjunctive or subject-verb agreement, may disrupt communication.

2. The performer has to be thinking about correctness, or be focused on form. Even when we have time, we may not be concerned with whether we have inflected the verb correctly! We may be more concerned with **what** we are saying and not **how** we are saying it. [9]

3. The performer has to know the rule. This is a very formidable requirement. Linguists readily admit that they have only been able to des-scribe a subset, a fragment, of the grammar of even well-studied languages such as English. We can assume that even the best students fail to learn everything presented to them.

The evidence for the performance model given in Figure One comes originally from the morpheme studies, although confirming evidence has been produced from other sources.[10]

Briefly, studies of the acquisition of grammatical morphemes using adult subjects have shown the following: we see the natural order for grammatical morphemes when we test students in situations that appear to be relatively "Monitor-free", where they are focused on communication and not form. When we give adult students pencil and paper grammar tests, we see "unnatural orders", a difficulty order that is unlike the child second language acquisition order. The interpretation of this result in terms of this theory is that when we focus students on communication, they are not usually able to make extensive use of their conscious knowledge of grammar, the Monitor, and their error patterns primarily reflect the operation of the acquired system. Since adult acquisition processes are posited to be similar to child language acquisition, the error patterns are similar to those seen in children. The unnatural order is due to the intrusion of conscious grammar in situations where students are deliberately focused on correctness. Specifically, the natural order is disturbed by the rise in accuracy of certain late acquired items, items that the performer has not yet acquired, but that are "easy" to learn (see below).

Current experimentation in this area has led to the hypothesis that in most cases a true grammar test is necessary to bring out the conscious grammar in force.[11] Even when students write compositions carefully, they may be so concerned with communication, with the message, that Monitor use may be light. This confirms the importance of requirement 2 described above.

A very important point about the Monitor Hypothesis is that it does not say that acquisition is unavailable for self-correction. We often self-correct, or edit, using acquisition, in both first and in second languages. What the Monitor Hypothesis claims is that conscious learning has only this function, that it is not used to initiate production in a second language.

The research also suggests that the Monitor does a better job with some parts of grammar than with others. Specifically, it seems to do better with rules that can be characterized as "simple" in two different ways. First, simple rules do not require elaborate or complex movements of permutation. An easy rule in this sense is the English third person singular, which only requires the attachment of a morpheme -s to the end of certain verbs. The French rule *de + le = du* is another example of a fairly simple morphological operation. Difficult rules in this sense include the English wh- question, which involves moving the questioned word to the front of the sentence, a subject-auxiliary inversion, and, with sentences having only main verbs, the insertion of *do*. Rules can also be difficult due to their semantic properties. The English article system is easy to describe formally — one inserts a *the* or *a* before the noun, but its semantics, i.e., when to use a determiner, are very difficult to describe.[12]

Monitor use is thus called for in the case of rules that are easy in both senses given above, and not yet acquired. The English third person singular, for example, is ideal for the conscious Monitor. It is relatively easy to describe and learn, and it is very late acquired, one of the last of the grammatical morphemes to arrive. In fact, even very advanced acquirers of English as a second language may miss the third person marker in unmonitored speech. If, however, they are efficient Monitor users, they will rarely get it wrong in writing, in prepared speech or on other occasions when monitoring is a relatively simple task.

The Input Hypothesis

This hypothesis states simply that we acquire (not learn) language by understanding input that is a little beyond our current level of (acquired) competence. This hypothesis is, in our opinion, of crucial importance since it attempts to answer a question that is important both theoretically and practically: How do we acquire language?

The Input Hypothesis claims that listening comprehension and reading are of primary importance in the language program, and that the ability to speak (or write) fluently in a second language will come on its own with time. Speaking fluency is thus not "taught" directly; rather, speaking ability "emerges" after the acquirer has built up competence through comprehending input.

The Input Hypothesis states that in order for acquirers to progress to the next stages in the acquisition of the target language, they need to understand input language that includes a structure that is part of the next stage. Thus, if the acquirers are "up to" the third person singular morpheme *-s* in English, they can only acquire this morpheme if they hear or read messages that utilize this structure and understand their meaning.

How do acquirers do this? How can we understand language that contains structures that we have not yet acquired? The answer is through context and extra-linguistic information. Caretakers provide this context for young children by restricting their talk to the "here and now", to what is in the child's domain at the moment. Good second language teachers do this by adding visual aids, by using extra-linguistic context. The Input Hypothesis thus claims that we use meaning to help us acquire language.

To state the hypothesis a bit more formally, an acquirer can "move" from a stage i (where i is the acquirer's level of competence) to a stage $i + 1$ (where $i + 1$ is the stage immediately following i along some natural order) by understanding language containing $i + 1$. This technical definition will be of use to us in later discussions. [13]

A corollary of the Input Hypothesis is the idea that input need not be finely tuned. Input does not have to aim only at $i+1$, the next step along the natural order. Returning to Figure One, if an English acquirer has acquired *-ing*, plural, and copula, and is "ready" to acquire auxiliary and articles, the teacher need not worry about providing auxiliary and articles in the input. In practice, providing optimal input may be surprisingly easy. It may be that all the teacher need do is make sure the students **understand** what is being said or what they are reading. When this happens, when the input is understood, if there is enough input, $i+1$ will usually be covered automatically. Other structures will of course be present in the input as well, but there will be plenty of exposure to the $i + 1$ as well as a review of previously acquired structures.

We refer to this as the **net**: when someone talks to you in a language you have not yet acquired completely (including your first language if you are a child) so that you understand what is said, the speaker "casts a net" of structure around your current level, your i. This net includes many instances of your $i+1$. Figure Two illustrates the difference between finely tuned input, input that aims specifically at one structure at a time, and roughly tuned input (the net), that is, the result of a speaker using a language so that the acquirer understands what is said.

FIGURE TWO
Finely-Tuned Input

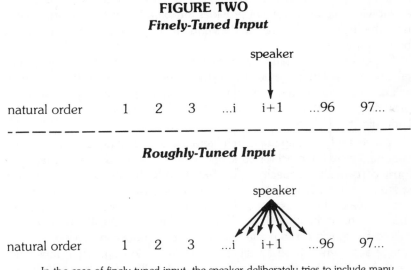

speaker

natural order   1   2   3   ...i   i+1   ...96   97...

Roughly-Tuned Input

speaker

natural order   1   2   3   ...i   i+1   ...96   97...

In the case of finely tuned input, the speaker deliberately tries to include many examples of the student's $i + 1$ (see text). In the case of roughly-tuned input, the speaker only attempts to make himself or herself understood. When this is accomplished, the speaker will automatically "cast a net" of structure that includes the acquirer's $i + 1$ (the net hypothesis).

Evidence for the Input Hypothesis and the related net hypothesis comes from a variety of sources, including reseach in child language acquisition and applied linguistics. The Input Hypothesis also fits very well with other phenomena and hypotheses about second language acquisition.

The existence and effect of caretaker speech on children provides good evidence for the Input Hypothesis as well as the concept of the net. Briefly, researchers have found that caretakers (mothers, fathers, and others) simplify their speech when they talk to children. This simplification is thought to be helpful for language acquisition: children acquiring second languages who get simplified input are assumed to acquire faster than those who do not. *Caretaker speech* has these very interesting properties:

1. It is motivated by the caretaker's desire to be understood. Caretakers modify their language in order to communicate, not in order to teach language! [14]

2. Caretaker speech is structurally simpler than the language adults use with each other. What is of interest to us is that it appears to be roughly tuned to the linguistic level of the child. Caretaker speech tends to get more complex as the child grows in linguistic maturity, although the relationship between the input complexity and the child's developing competence is not perfect.

3. Caretaker speech is about the here and now. Adults do not discuss tomorrow's party, next week's trip, or what is happening down the street, with very young children. As the children grow in linguistic competence, the input becomes more displaced in time and space. We interpret this finding as showing that the caretaker provides the extra-linguistic support, or context, that helps the children understand language that may be "a little bit beyond them". [15]

The description of caretaker speech thus fits the input hypothesis: caretakers "teach" language by altering their language to children so that they will be understood. In doing so, they are giving optimal language lessons, providing input that is understandable and that "covers" the child's next linguistic stage.

The second language research literature tells us that second language acquirers may have access to simple caretaker-like speech as well. One form of caretaker speech is *foreigner talk,* the modifications native speakers make when talking to non-native speakers. These modifications are motivated by the same forces that motivate caretaker speech: communication. Researchers have documented many of the things those who talk to foreigners do to make things easier to understand for second language acquirers. These modifications include: slowing down, repeating, restating, changing *wh-* questions to *yes/no* questions (e.g. from: *Where are you going?* to *Are you going home?* The second question requires only *yes* or *no.* [16]) The complexity of foreigner talk also appears to be roughly tuned to the level of the acquirer. [17]

Teacher talk is foreigner talk in the second language classroom. It is the language of classroom management and explanation, when it is in the target language. There is good evidence that teacher talk is also roughly tuned to the level of the acquirer.[18] Teacher talk as well is motivated by the desire to communicate. It may thus be the case that "caretaker speech" is available to adult second language acquirers and that it has approximately the same effect on them as it does on children.

Most classroom exercises in grammar-based approaches attempt to be finely tuned; teacher talk will most likely be roughly tuned. If the Input Hypothesis is correct, however, teacher talk is actually more valuable! When we "just talk" to our students, **if they understand**, we are not only giving a language lesson, we may be giving the best possible language lesson since we will be supplying input for acquisition. Roughly tuned input has several real advantages over finely-tuned exercises: with rough tuning, we are always assured that $i+1$ will be covered, while with finely tuned exercises, we are taking a guess as to where the student is. With roughly tuned input, we are assured of constant recycling and review; this is not the case with "lock-step" exercises. Third, roughly tuned input will be good for more than one acquirer at a time, even when they are at slightly different levels. Finally, roughly tuned caretaker-like speech in the form of teacher talk or foreigner talk, will nearly always be more interesting than an exercise that focuses just on one grammatical point.

Another form of simple input available to the second language acquirers is the speech of other second language acquirers. This **interlanguage talk** might be very useful for language acquisition: it is certainly meant for real communication, and might even contain enough input at an acquirer's $i+1$ to help him or her acquire beyond the current level. It remains, however, an empirical question whether the possible advantages of interlanguage talk balance the obvious problems: the ungrammaticality of much of the input, and the possibility that the input might be too simple and not be progressive enough for the intermediate or advanced acquirer.

Aspects of Second Language Acquisition Related to the Input Hypothesis

The Input Hypothesis is consistent with other phenomena in second language acquisition. First it helps to account for what may be called the **silent period** in informal second language acquisition. It has often been observed, especially with children acquiring a second language, that for several months following the first exposure the acquirer may say very little except for memorized whole sentences (routines and patterns; see discussion below). Hatch in a 1972 study, for example, reported that Paul, a five-year-old acquirer of English as a second language, did not really begin to speak for several months after he came to the United States. His only early output was memorized sentences such as *Get out of here. It's time to eat and drink.* which he clearly learned as whole utterances without a real understanding of their components (e.g. he would probably not understand the words *"out"* or *"time"* if they were used in other sentences). When "real" language did start to emerge, it looked very much like normal first language development, with short, simple word combinations such as, *this kite, ball no.* Other researchers have reported similar phenomena.[19]

The silent period may be the time during which acquirers build up competence by active listening, via input. In accordance with the input hypothesis, speaking ability emerges after enough competence has been developed by listening and understanding. We should note that the case histories dealing with children acquiring second languages agree that at least several months may elapse until they start talking, and that this early speech is not error-free. These facts have important pedagogical considerations, as we shall see later.

There is also some evidence from applied linguistics research which supports the Input Hypothesis. Earlier research which attempted to compare methodologies in an effort to see which one is "best", that is, which one produces the fastest achievement in the second languages, did not yield strong results. In several studies, cognitive-oriented teaching methods were compared to audiolingual methods, and only minor differences emerged. The results of these method comparison studies can be summarized as follows:

1. Differences between the methods are never very large, but are occasionally statistically significant.

2. Deductive methods, such as cognitive-code, are more effective for older students (adults). (See footnote 1 for discussion of "deductive" and "inductive.")

3. There is no difference between methods for adolescents.

4. Methods emphasizing written skills (grammar-translation) produce better results for reading and writing, while methods emphasizing oral-aural skills (audiolingual) produce slighly better results for speaking and listening.[20]

Our view is that none of the methods used, audiolingual, grammar-translation, or other cognitive approaches, all of which are grammar-based, produces optimal input for language acquisition, since they are designed primarily for learning.

There are some recent method comparisons, however, that claim far more spectacular results: a series of studies have been published over the last few years that have several characteristics in common:

1. They compare methods that focus on providing comprehensible input, input in which the focus is on the message not the grammatical form.

2. They allow a silent period during which speech is delayed or optional. Students do not have to talk until they are ready.

3. In all cases, the students using these input methods do **much** better than in either audiolingual or cognitive-oriented control groups.

A good example are Asher's studies comparing students taught with a traditional grammar-type approach and students taught using his **Total Physical Response** techniques. In Total Physical Response, students are required to obey the instructor's commands, given in the target language. These commands require a "total physical response", beginning with simple imperatives *Sit down!* and leading to more complex sentences, *If John ran to the blackboard, run after him and hit him with your book.* Asher maintains that an enormous amount of grammar can be embedded in the input in this way. Students are not forced to talk in the early stages and only start producing (in the form of commands to the teacher!) after about 10 hours of input. In a 1972 study, students of German as a foreign language (adult night school class), after only 32 hours of total physical response study of German, outperformed controls who had had 150 hours of college German on a test of listening comprehension and did just as well as the controls on other skills. This is nearly five times the acquisition rate! Asher has produced similar results for different languages and different settings in many other experiments, including studies of English as a second language, and studies using children as well as adults. [21]

Swaffer and Woodruff's study in 1978 at the University of Texas is another instructive example. The students (German as a foreign language) used total physical response for the first four weeks of the semester with the rest of the year emphasizing listening comprehension, reading comprehension for content, and only limited grammar covering features considered "essential for listening and reading." They found that their students scored well above the national norms on standard tests (Modern Language Association), more students continued on to German II than in previous years and evaluations of the classes were much higher than in previous years. [22]

The Input Hypothesis is summarized in Table Three. We have spent more time with it that some of the other hypotheses because of its crucial importance to pedagogy, and we will return to it on several occasions.

TABLE THREE
The Input Hypothesis: Major Points

1. Relates to acquisition, not to learning.
2. We acquire by understanding language a bit beyond our current level of competence. This is done with the help of context.
3. Spoken fluency emerges gradually and is not taught directly.
4. When caretakers talk to acquirers so that the acquirers understand the message, input automatically contains "i+1", the grammatical structures the acquirer is "ready" to acquire.

The Affective Filter Hypothesis

This hypothesis states that **attitudinal** variables relating to success in second language acquisition generally relate directly to language acquisition but not necessarily to language learning.

The research literature indicates that certain **affective variables** are related to second language achievement. Performers with certain types of motivation, usually , but not always "integrative" [23] and with good self-images do better in second language acquisition. Also, the best situations for language acquisition seem to be those which encourage lower anxiety levels.

The reason affective factors are hypothesized to be directly related to acquisition is that, in general, they appear to relate strongly to second language achievement when communicative-type tests are used, tests that involve the acquired rather than the learned system, and when the students taking the test have encountered the language in "acquisition-rich" situations, i.e., second language acquisition in the country rather than foreign language learning exclusively in a traditional classroom. [24]

Dulay and Burt have suggested that attitudinal factors may relate to second language acquisition in the following way: performers with optimal attitudes have a lower **affective filter.** A low filter means that the performer is more "open" to the input, and that the input strikes "deeper", to use Stevick's term. Thus, having the right attitudes may do two things for second language acquirers: it will encourage them to try to get more input, to interact with speakers of the target language with confidence, and also to be more receptive to the input they get. [25] Figure Three represents the affective filter and how it relates to second language acquisition.

To summarize, we have hypothesized that certain attitudinal variables relate primarily to subconscious language acquisition, and that they have two effects: (1) they actually encourage input; people who are motivated and who have a positive self-image will seek and obtain more input; (2) they contribute to a lower filter; given two acquirers with the exact same input, the one with a lower filter will acquire more. The second effect is of great importance to the acquirer in a classroom setting; it implies that our pedagogical goals should not only include supplying optimal input, but also creating a situation that promotes a low filter. We shall see that most of the practices of the Natural Approach are designed to do just these two things — supply good comprehensible input and lower the affective filter.

These five hypotheses form the core of the second language acquisition theory that underlies the Natural Approach. In the second part of this chapter, we consider the implication of the theory to several issues — second language "aptitude", first language "interference" in second language performance, the role of routines and patterns, individual variation, and age differences in second language rate and attainment.

FIGURE THREE
Operation of the "Affective Filter"

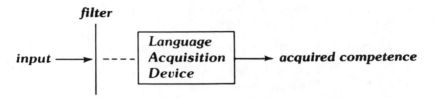

The affective filter acts to prevent input from being used for language acquisition. Acquirers with optimal attitudes (see text) are hypothesized to have a low affective filter. Classrooms that encourage low filters are those that promote low anxiety among students, that keep students off the defensive.[26]

FACTORS WHICH INFLUENCE SECOND LANGUAGE ACQUISITION

Second Language Aptitude

There has been considerable interest over the last two decades in the idea of second language **aptitude.** Some individuals, it is believed, have a special aptitude for second language study. These students are thought to be the ones who should pursue language study and who can be expected to make the most rapid progress in second language classes.

There is considerable empirical support for this idea. Many studies have shown that students who do better on Language Aptitude Tests such as Carroll and Sapon's *Modern Language Aptitude Test* or Pimsleur's *Language Aptitude Battery* do, in fact, perform better in foreign language classes.[27] There are several reasons for hypothesizing, however, that the kind of linguistic competence tapped by aptitude tests is language learning and not language acquisition.

First, aptitude tests predict speed of learning in foreign language classes. Achievement in foreign language classes is usually measured by grammar-type tests that involve heavy use of conscious grammar rules, i.e., the Monitor. Several empirical studies confirm that aptitude measures relate to "classroom skills" better than they relate to "communication skills".[28] Also, the aptitude tests themselves consist to a large extent of tasks that require a conscious awareness of language. In the Pimsleur battery, for example, testees are asked to analyze sentences in a foreign language unknown to them and to work out the generalizations, or rules, so that they can judge whether additional sentences in the language are grammatical. The following is a typical example:[29]

> The examinee is given a number of forms in a foreign language (Kabardian) and their English equivalents. From these, he must

conclude how other things are said in this language...Sample:

shi gader le = the horse sees father
shi gader la = the horse saw father
be = carries

Q. How do you say "The horse carried father"?

1. shi gader be
2. shi gader ba
3. gade shir be
4. gade shir ba

Success on items like this requires inductive language learning ability, the ability to consciously "figure out" rules of grammar.[30] It does not involve language acquisiton. Language acquistion, we have hypothesized, requires the comprehension of meaningful input, and is slowly built up after many exposures. The result of inductive language learning is a conscious rule, which is what the example from the Pimsleur test demands. The result of language acquisition is a "feel" for grammaticality and an ability to use a rule in real communication.

Hypothesizing that aptitude relates to learning and attitude to language acquisition has several interesting consequences. First, it solves a problem in theory of second language acquisition: how can attitude and aptitude both be related to achievement in second languages, yet be unrelated to each other (we see students with high aptitude and low attitude, low aptitude and high attitude, low on both, and high on both!)? The answer is that they relate to different means of developing ability in second languages: acquisition and learning. Another consequence is a practical one: if acquisition is more central, more important than learning, this implies that attitudinal factors are more important in second language acquisition than aptitude. Having high aptitude makes you a good learner but not necessarily a good acquirer. This may be an asset but it is certainly not sufficient for success in second language acquisition. On the other hand, a high aptitude does seem to predict success in a language classroom which is grammar-based and on tests that demand grammatical analysis rather than real communicative ability.

The Role of the First Language

The role of the first language in second language performance is often referred to as **interference.** This implies that our knowledge of our first language actually gets in the way when we try to speak a second language. If true, this means that we need to fight off this interference. Indeed, this is what many exercises attempt to do: they provide extra practice and drill on just those structures in which the first and second languages differ.

Our view of first language interference is quite different, and it implies a very different cure for interference errors. The research supports an idea first proposed by Newmark, who suggested that the first language does not interfere at all when we try to use a second language. Rather, errors that show the influence of the first language are simply the result of "falling back" on the first language when we lack a rule in our second language. The cure for interference is simply acquisition — pedagogy does not need to help the acquirer fight off the effects of the first language — it need only help the acquirer acquire the target language. [31]

Stated more formally, an acquirer will substitute some first language rule for a rule of the second language if the acquirer needs the rule to express himself but has not yet acquired it. The L1 rule used may be quite similar to the L2 rule, but may also differ in certain ways. When the L1 and L2 rules are different, the resulting error is often referred to as interference. But according to Newmark, it is not interference at all; it is not the result of the first language interfering with the second language performance, but the result of ignorance — the lack of acquisition of a target language rule that is needed in performance.

Here is an example: pretend you are a student in a German class, and you have been given a few rules of German and some vocabulary. The teacher then asks you to speak, to say something in German. Since there has been insufficient time and insufficient input to acquire German word order, your only recourse will be to use English word order, the "surface structure" of English. The process may go like this: You wish to say *I am happy to be here.* You first use the English order and then insert German words: *Ich bin glücklich zu sein hier. 'I am happy to be here.'*

Your German "Monitor", your conscious knowledge of German may be able to make small repairs (remember that the use of the conscious Monitor is limited to rules that are "easy"). For example, you many consciously know that *sein* is the infinitive form in German and that in sentences with modal verbs, the main verb is placed at the end of the sentence: *Ich bin glücklich hier zu sein.* In this case the output is grammatically correct. In other cases, however, the rules are more complex and not easily monitored: the result is error. Suppose, for example, the beginning students wish to say in Spanish, *'I don't have it.'* If they produce the Spanish lexical items with English word order, they will have *Yo no tengo lo,* assuming they can correctly Monitor rules for the first person singular of the verb and apply negation correctly. But a movement transformation in Spanish places the object pronoun in preverbal position: *Yo no lo tengo.* Experienced instructors report that this is a very difficult sort of rule for beginners to Monitor with ease.

We refer to this mode of producing sentences as the **L1 plus Monitor Mode.** [32] It involves no acquired competence, and has both advantages and disadvantages. The advantages are short term, however, while the disadvantages in the long run appear to be serious.

One obvious advantage is that the use of an L1 rule allows performers to "outperform their competence", to meet a practical need in communication in the target language before they have acquired the relevant $i + 1$ rule. When the L1 rule used is identical to a rule in the L2 ("positive transfer"), performers seem to have gotten something for free. Even if the L1 rule is not the same as the L2 rule, one could argue that performers still come out ahead, as, quite often, they can still communicate their point despite the incorrect form.

Another advantage is that the early production allowed by the use of L1 rules also helps to invite output — it allows the performer to participate more in conversation, and this could mean more comprehensible input and thus more second language acquisition. [33]

There are real disadvantages to falling back on the L1, however. First, the L1 rule may not be the same as an L2 rule, as noted above, and errors can result. The conscious Monitor can note and repair these errors in some cases, but not all, since, as we have seen, the constraints on Monitor use are severe. Thus, use of L1 rules requires constant vigilance on the part of the Monitor. Second, this is an extremely awkward and tiring way to produce formally correct sentences in a second language. It requires an immense amount of mental gymnastics that most people are not capable of. In addition, Monitor correction of such errors will not, according to the theory, produce acquisition, or permanent change. It will not eradicate the first language rule, even if done effectively over long periods of time. Real acquisition comes only from comprehensible input.

First language interference thus occurs when the second language performers have to talk "too early," before they have had the time and input to build enough competence to use acquired competence. Along with routines and patterns, which we will discuss below, it can be a short-term solution to early speech demands.

Early production may be useful in second language situations, where the student is actually in the country and needs the second language for communication right away. In such cases, the advantages of the L1 plus Monitor Mode might outweigh the disadvantages. In foreign language situations, however, we have the luxury of waiting for acquired competence to build up via input, and a great deal of first language "transfer" can be avoided.

Routines and Patterns

Routines and patterns are sentences that are memorized wholes or partially memorized wholes. Examples of routines are sentences like: *What's your name? Parlez-vous français?* spoken by performers who have not acquired or learned the rules involved. For example, someone who used the second example might not have any idea that *parlez* meant *"speak"*. Patterns are partially memorized sentences with an empty "slot" for a noun or noun phrase. The tourist who asks: *Where is the......?* where the blank could be filled with *opera, police station, Grand Hotel,* etc. is using a pattern.

Krashen and Scarcella argue that routines and patterns are neither acquisition nor learning, nor do they turn into acquisition or learning directly, except to occasionally serve as comprehensible input. [34]

Informal second language acquirers often make extensive use of routines and patterns in early stages as a means of saying things before their acquired competence is ready. Hatch's Paul, discussed earlier, did not speak English for several months after his arrival in the United States, except for a few routines that were undoubtedly highly useful for a five-year-old, such as *"Get out of here."* An adult informal acquirer, Fatmah, studied by Hanania and Gradman used mainly "memorized items that are commonly used in social contexts with children" during her first few months in the United States. She used phrases such as *I can't...Do you like ...?* as patterns, but according to Hanania and Gradman had not acquired the rules for productive use of the items in the patterns, i.e., she could not use verbs like *can* in other sentences. [35]

Given enough comprehensible input, acquisition usually "catches up" with the routines and patterns of the informal acquirer. Speakers like Paul and Fatmah were eventually able to use their acquired competence in their second language to produce the same sentences that they had at one time required routines and patterns for.

Even though routines and patterns are not of direct benefit to language acquisition or to language learning, they may be of considerable indirect benefit. [36] As we remarked in discussing the L1 plus Monitor Mode, this "premature" kind of output does allow early production and thus invites input. This early production may also come in handy in situations where we cannot afford to wait for acquisition to produce fluent speech: the immigrant may need to say *My stomach hurts* to the doctor and it is of little consequence whether that utterance was produced by the acquired system or by a routine or pattern. Correctly used, routines and patterns can help acquirers gain more input and "manage conversations": it helps to know from the start how to say *Excuse me. What does .... mean?* and *just a moment* or the equivalent in any target language.

On the other hand, routines and patterns can lead to trouble. The tourist who asks *Where is the opera?* may get a complete answer! (*You go straight for two blocks, then turn right, go until you come to a gas station. . . .*). In other words, routines and patterns may get you in over your head. (There are ways around this. One is to ask yes/no questions: *Is the opera this way?*). Another problem with routines and patterns is familiar to many dialog learners: we often have to run through the entire dialog to get our line! Finally, effective use of routines and dialogs requires having a "line" ready when the situation arises: the situation you are prepared for may not come up, or worse yet, you may not have a line for every situation!

Individual Variation

The theory of second language acquisition described here posits a basic uniformity in language acquisition: "deep down," we all acquire language in the same way, via comprehensible input. This is not to say, however, that individual variation does not exist. It does, and the theory makes specific predictions about it. It predicts that acquirers will vary only in certain ways and not in others. We will not see individual variation in the acquisition process itself, for example. Also, the Natural Order Hypothesis and the Monitor Hypothesis will hold for everyone.

We do, however, see variation in the rate and extent of acquisition. The theory predicts that this is due to one or both of two factors: the amount of comprehensible input an acquirer obtains, and the strength of the affective filter. We can also see variation with respect to the extent to which a performer utilizes routines and patterns. Peters hypothesizes that such variation in first language acquisition is due to the type of input the child is exposed to: children who receive less caretaker speech develop more formulaic output. [37]

Our focus in this section is individual variation in Monitor use. There appear to be basically three types of adult second language acquirers.

1. Monitor **over-users** are those who monitor all the time. Monitor over-users are constantly checking their output with their learned conscious knowledge of the second language. As a result, they speak hesitantly, often self-correct in the middle of utterances, and are so concerned with correctness that they have difficulty speaking with any real fluency. There may be two causes for over-use of the Monitor. Over-use may derive from learning without acquisition. Someone who has only had formal exposure to a second language in grammar-based classes may have very little acquisition to rely on and may have no choice but to be an over-user. Another type may be related to personality. These over-users are people who have acquired at least some of the grammar of their second language but have no faith in their acquired competence. Such performers may be like "S", described by Stafford and Covitt; they noted that "S", an English acquirer, spoke very little "because she tried to remember and use grammar rules before speaking." [38]

2. Monitor **under-users** are second language performers who do not seem to use the Monitor to any extent, even when conditions encourage it. Such performers, like first language acquirers, appear to be uninfluenced by most error correction. Under-users, when they do self-correct, do so "by feel," by the way it "sounds." One under-user, "I," also studied by Stafford and Covitt, remarked that even in writing ". . . *first of all I listen to myself as it sounds. I mean I write it and then I see if it sounds correct.*" Under-users do not rely on conscious rules, but only on acquisition. Despite this, many under-users pay "lip-service" to the value of conscious grammar. "I" felt that people need conscious rules to speak "correctly", and Stafford and

Covitt point out that under-users often feel "grammar is the key to every language", even if they hardly use, consciously, any of the rules themselves.

3. The **optimal** Monitor user is the adult second language performer who uses the Monitor when it is appropriate, when it does not get in the way of communication. In normal conversation, where the focus is on communication and when there is little time, the optimal user will not be excessively concerned with applying conscious rules to performance. In writing, and in planned speech, when there is time, optimal users will make whatever corrections possible to raise the accuracy of their output.

Optimal Monitor users can therefore use their learned competence as a supplement to their acquired competence. We often see second language performers who have acquired a great deal of the second language but still make occasional errors in casual speech, especially in late-acquired morphology (e.g. the third person singular ending on regular verbs in English, or gender agreement in noun phrases of many languages, Spanish, French, German, etc.) These advanced performers can use conscious grammar to correct these items when they write, and often their written production appears to be quite native-like.

The goal of the Natural Approach is to produce optimal Monitor users, performers who put conscious grammar in its proper place. An over-emphasis on conscious grammar has the undesirable result of encouraging over-use of the Monitor. But completely eliminating grammar robs our students of the chance to use conscious learning as a supplement to acquisition. If our observations about individual variation are correct, they imply that formal grammar instruction does not have a central place in the curriculum, but it does have an important role to play.

Age Differences

Another issue that the theory of second language acquisition presented here helps to explain is the question of age differences in second language acquisition. Before attempting to explain age differences, let us first review the research on the effect of age on second language acquisition.

Contrary to popular opinion, it is not simply the case that "younger is better," that children are better than adults in all respects in second language acquisition. Rather, children are "better" with respect to **ultimate attainment**; over the long run, those who start second languages as children will usually reach higher levels of competence than those who start as adults (i.e. after age 15). Over the short run, however, adults are **faster** in attaining second language proficiency than younger children.[39] Thus, any explanation of age differences must account for why children excel in ultimate attainment and why adults are faster, at least in early stages.

Older acquirers may be superior in initial rate of acquisition because they are able to get more comprehensible input. There appear to be at least three ways this happens. First, as Scarcella and Higa's research shows, older acquirers are better at "managing conversations", or controlling the input directed at them and making it comprehensible.[40] Scarcella and Higa studied child (ages 8.5 and 9.5) and adolescent (ages 15.5 and 16.5) acquirers of English as a second language engaged in a block-building task with native speakers of English. They report that although the younger acquirers received what appeared to be simpler input, the older acquirers were much more adept at managing the conversation and at getting the native speaker to modify the input. The adolescents were better at keeping the conversation going and at getting the native speaker to be more comprehensible ("negotiating meaning"). They would, for example, ask for help and change the topic more than younger acquirers. Thus, despite the child's simpler input, the adolescent may actually receive more comprehensible input, and this may be largely responsible for their greater speed of acquisition.

A second factor contributing to older acquirers' greater speed in initial stages is their greater ability to "beat the silent period", to produce in the second language using structures that have not yet been acquired. This is done by using first language rules and relying on the Monitor for repair, as described earlier. This practice allows older performers to "outperform their competence." Since the use of the L1 plus the Monitor facilitates early production, it also invites input; clearly, the more you talk, the more others can and will talk to you. As we mentioned earlier, however, use of this mode has definite drawbacks, in that it requires constant attention to form, constant mental gymnastics.

A third reason for the older acquirer's rate superiority in initial stages is the fact that older acquirers have a greater knowledge of the world. This greater extra-linguistic knowledge helps make input comprehensible. The same message delivered to an eight-year old and to a 28-year old of equal linguistic competence may be much more comprehensible to the latter, thanks to the greater amount of background information and experience possessed by the older acquirer.

The child's eventual superiority in second language acquisition is hypothesized to be due to affective factors. Specifically, we hypothesize that the affective filter increases in strength at around puberty.

It was hypothesized earlier in this chapter that affective variables have two effects on second language acquisition: people with the "right" attitudes (high motivation, self confidence, low anxiety) will be more prone to interaction and thus get more input, and will also have a lower affective filter: they will let the input "in" for further language acquisition.

Puberty may be the turning point for ultimate success in second language acquisition, and there is good reason to hypothesize that it is at puberty that the affective filter increases in strength dramatically.[41] While affective variables do have an effect on second langage acquisition before puberty, they do not seem to be strong enough to limit ultimate attainment in children; given sufficient exposure, most children reach native-like levels of competence in second languages.

What are the affective changes that take place at puberty? Why do we hypothesize that the filter is strengthened at this time? Puberty, for those readers who do not remember, is often a time of emotional upheaval, a time of hypersensitivity and self-consciousness. Elkind describes these changes in some detail: adolescents are often self-centered, and preoccupied with their own appearance and behavior. They anticipate the reactions of other people, believing that they are the center of attention at all times. This leads to the feeling that they are under "the constant scrutiny of other people", and results in a reluctance to reveal oneself and feelings of vulnerability. Elkind suggests that Piaget's formal operations stage, in addition to biological puberty, may contribute to this change: the adolescents' increased ability to think abstractly allows them to better conceptualize other people's thoughts. Adolescents, however, make the error of thinking that other people are as concerned about their behavior as they are. This adds to the hypersensitivity and self-consciousness typical of this age group.[42]

Hypothesizing that the filter gains significantly in strength in early adolescence makes some very specific claims about age differences: first, it claims that there is no fundamental change in the language acquisition process at puberty. The ability to acquire does not disappear at puberty nor is it seriously damaged; rather, the necessary input is often blocked and therefore is less available for acquisition.

The filter explanation of child-adult differences in attainment relates attainment differences to acquisition and not to learning. It hypothesizes that over the long run the child will acquire more, not learn more. It should be pointed out, however, that the differences we see in ultimate attainment are in some cases not large, and there are adults who do extremely well in second language acquisition. The child will have a better chance of appearing to be a native speaker of a second language, but this does not imply that the adult beginner cannot attain very high levels of proficiency. The increase in filter strength may only mean that most adults will probably not attain a native-like level: the acquisition process is hypothesized to be very strong, and the filter, if successfully lowered, may only prevent the final stages of second language acquisition for many acquirers, the final few yards of a mile-long journey.

This hypothesis does not even exclude the possibility that some adult beginners may in fact eventually achieve native levels of proficiency. It would predict, however, that such acquirers would have access to sufficient amounts of comprehensible input, and would possess certain personality characteristics associated with a low affective filter and/or would have the opportunity to acquire the language in circumstances encouraging a low filter. Also many excellent performers can attain the illusion of achieving a native level with optimal Monitor use.

Notes

1. As discussed in Chapter One, giving learners rules and then asking them to practice the rules is generally referred to as deductive teaching, while encouraging students to discover rules on their own is called inductive teaching. A fair amount of research has investigated which type is best, and there is evidence for individual variation according to learning style (Seliger 1975; Krashen 1975). Both deductive and inductive rule learning are types of conscious learning; neither is acquisition.

2. This works fine in theory, but it is not clear that error correction has this desirable effect in actual practice. See papers by Fanselow 1977; Long 1977; and Cohen and Robbins 1976.

3. Brown 1973; Brown and Hanlon 1970; Brown, Cazden, and Bellugi 1973.

4. See for example Lawler and Selinker 1971; Corder 1967; and Bialystok 1979.

5. See de Villers and de Villiers 1973. A cross-sectional study is done at one point in time, while a longitudinal study is done over a long period. Cross-sectional studies typically involve large numbers of subjects and seek to determine difficulty order rather than acquisition order. While longitudinal studies generally use fewer subjects (sometimes just one), they are enormously time consuming, sometimes lasting a year or longer. Longitudinal studies are more valid than cross-sectional studies in determining acquisition order in that they measure the order of acquisition directly, and it is not always the case that cross-sectional results concur with longitudinal results.

6. Dulay and Burt 1973, 1974, 1975. See Fabris 1978; Makino 1978; Kessler and Idar 1977 for replications. Hakuta 1976 is a notable exception and is discussed in Krashen 1981.

7. Adult studies confirming the natural order include Andersen 1976; Kayfetz-Fuller 1978. Christison 1979; Long 1981; Krashen, Houck, Giunchi, Bode, Birnbaum and Strei 1977.

8. There is considerable evidence for a natural order for other stuctures in English (Krashen, Sferlazza, Feldman, and Fathman 1976; Keyfetz-Fuller 1978) as well as for structures in other languages (Snow and Hoefnagel-Hohle 1978). Also, at least two studies have found agreement among acquirers for difficulty order of grammatical structures in comprehension tasks (Morsback 1981; d'Anglejan and Tucker 1975).

   Morpheme studies are limited in several ways. The studies discussed in the text are limited to an analysis of the items in "obligatory occasions." They ask only: Does the acquirer use the morpheme correctly in places it is called for? A morpheme is scored as "correct" if it is supplied where required, and is scored as not correct if omitted, e.g., *He goes to work every day* is correct. *He go . . to work every day* is not. (In some studies, partial credit is allowed for a "misformed" morpheme in the correct obligatory occasion.) This means that some interesting phenomena, such as overgeneralization, the use of morphemes in places where they should not be, as in *I goes to work every day* are not covered by the morpheme studies. Second, the morpheme studies discussed here only show us the actual order of acquisition of the items involved. They do not show us the path the acquirer took in getting to the final form, the errors he or she made en route, the "intermediate" or "transitional" forms. The study of transitional forms is fascinating. For example, it has been found that language acquirers (first and second, child and adult) pass through fairly predictable "stages" in the acquisition of negation. Typically, they first negate sentences by placing a negative marker (such as "no") outside. For *The sun isn't shining* a young child might say *No the sun is shining*. In a later stage the acquirer typically puts the negative marker between the subject and the verb, as in *I no want envelope*. In this stage acquirers often use the word *don't* for negation, which sounds just like correct native speaker use, as in *You don't want some supper*. There is good evidence, however, that the acquirers are using *don't* as an equivalent for *no*, that is, it does not have the meaning of *do + negative*, as it does in native speaker speech. Finally, in later stages, the negative system approaches the native speaker standard, and *don't* is "re-analysed." For research in child language acquisiton on negation, see especially Klima and Bellugi, 1966; Bloom 1970; and Lord 1974. For second language acquisiton, see Cancino, Rosansky, and Schumann 1978; and especially Schumann's excellent review paper (Schumann 1978). (It should be pointed out also that there is some controversy as to whether early negation as described above, with the negative marker outside the sentence, always exists.) These limitations of the morpheme studies do not invalidate them, but show that they represent only a part of language acquisition.

9. Dulay and Burt 1977, 1978. In a very recent study of English speaking adults acquiring Dutch as a second language in Holland, Hulstijn (1982) reported that focussing on form required more time of subjects. Simply adding "time pressure," however, did not significantly affect accuracy in form. This suggests that the "time condition" may not be as central as the "focus on form" condition, and that the relationship between focus and form and time may be as follows: focussing on form, or being concerned about correctness, takes time, and this extra time can disrupt conversation.
10. See the work of Bialystock and Frohlich 1977, 1978a, 1978b and Bialystock 1979.
11. Keyfetz 1978; Houck, Robertson and Krashen 1978; Krashen, Butler, Birnbaum and Robertson 1978.
12. See, for example, Hawkins 1978.
13. Comprehension of input may be necessary for language acquisition but may not be sufficient: We can understand input and still not acquire. There are several reasons for stating this restriction of the input hypothesis. First, there may be an affective filter, a "block" that prevents comprehended input from being used for futher language acquisition. This possibility will be discussed below. Also, it is quite possible to understand without making any form-function connection. Research in psycholinguistics has shown that we often "by-pass" syntactic structure in understanding sentences. (Bever, 1970; Tarone, 1974). Related to this is the fact that we can often "get the gist" of what someone is saying, even though the actual utterance is far beyond our current level of competence and far beyond our $i + 1$.
14. See Clark and Clark 1977 and Newport, Gleitman, and Gleitman 1975.
15. See Cross 1975 and Newport, Gleitman and Gleitman 1975.
16. Hatch, Shapira and Gough 1978.
17. See e.g. Freed 1980.
18. See Gaies 1977 and the discussion in Krashen 1981.
19. See for example Hakuta 1974 and Ervin-Tripp 1975.
20. For a review of these studies, see Krashen 1982a.
21. See for example, Asher 1965, 1966; Asher and Price 1967; Asher and Garcia 1969; Asher 1969; Asher, Kusudo and De la Torre 1974; and Asher 1979.
22. For a review of other relevant studies, see Gary and Gary 1980.
23. Integrative motivation refers to the desire to "be like" speakers of the target language. In foreign language situations (e.g. studying French in Anglophone Canada), students with more integrative motivations are usually superior, especially over the long run (Gardner and Lambert 1972). In situations where there is some urgency in second language acquisition and/or where there is less desire to integrate, the presence of integrative motivation may not relate to second language achievement. Rather, instrumental motivation, the desire to use the language for practical means, may predict success better (Lukami 1972; Gardner and Lambert 1972; Oller, Baca, and Vigil 1977). See also Heyde 1977; Krashen 1981 contains a review of the relevant issues.
24. Krashen, 1981.
25. Dulay and Burt, 1977.
26. This apt term is from Stevick 1976.
27. Correlations of aptitude test scores and foreign language achievement are always positive, usually significant, but not always substantial. Pimsleur reports the following: The MLAT (Modern Language Aptitude Test) was correlated against course grades of eighteen groups of French, Spanish, and German students, in grades 9 to 11. The eighteen validity coefficients ranged from .25 to .78: the median group of junior high school students yielded a coefficient of .71 (Pimsleur 1966, p. 1981).
These results appear to be typical.
28. See especially Gardner, Smythe, Clement and Gliksman 1976 and Gardner and Lambert 1972.
29. Pimsleur 1966.
30. It should be pointed out that not all subcomponents of aptitude tests relate directly to language learning. Krashen concludes that two of the three components of aptitude identified by Carroll relate directly to learning: inductive ability and grammatical sensitivity. The other component is phonetic ability, which is beyond the scope of this discussion (See Krashen 1981 and Carroll 1973).

31. Newmark 1966. For reviews see Krashen 1981, 1982.
32. Several scholars have pointed out that this view of transfer is too strong in that it predicts the occurrence of "transfer" errors that in fact do not occur. This problem can be resolved by positing several constraints on transfer, or conditions that must be met before a performer can substitute a first language rule for some i + 1.

    Zobl (1980a, b, c) notes that the first language rule itself must be a productive one. This accounts for the fact that French speakers acquiring English as a second language do not make errors like *John comes he?* after the French *Jean vient-il?* The French rule, according to Zobl, is no longer productive in French. Citing Terry 1970, Zobl notes that it is mainly limited to present tense contexts, an indication that the rule is becoming unproductive.

    Kellerman 1978 provides another condition on transfer: the performer must perceive the transferred rule to be potentially non-language specific. Kellerman's original experiments in lexical transfer showed that foreign language students were less willing to transfer features of words they considered to be less "core." For example, a Dutch speaking student of English would be more likely to presume that he could transfer the Dutch verb 'brechen' (break) in an English sentence *He broke his leg,* than in *The waves broke on the shore.* A similar constraint exists in syntax. Dutch students of English, Kellerman reports, were not willing to accept a literal translation into English of the Dutch equivalent of *The book reads well,* apparently because the intrasitive use of *read* was perceived to be language-specific and infrequent (see also Jordans and Kellerman 1978).

    Another constraint comes from the work of Wode 1978, and accounts for the findings that L1 influenced errors do not seem to occur at all stages of the acquirer's development. Wode states that for an interlinguistic error to occur, the L1 rule and the L2 rule it substitutes for must meet a "crucial similarity measure" (p. 116). In other words, if an L1 rule is to be utilized, it must be preceded by the acquisition of some i of the L2 that differs from it only in minimal ways. Wode's example, from child second language acquisition of English by German speakers, illustrates this point nicely. Wode notes that errors such as *John go not to school* occur, in which German-like post-verbal negation is used. These errors are not found in beginning acquirers, but occur, according to Wode, only after the acquirer has reached the "aux-negation" stage and already produces sentences such as *John can not go.* The acquirer then overgeneralizes the negative rule from post-auxiliary to post-verbal, and uses the first language rule.
33. There is another way in which use of the L1 may indirectly help second language acquisition. The existence of cognates will help to make input comprehensible, even if form and meaning are not identical across the languages. This factor will increase the rate of acquisition but not alter the order.
34. Krashen and Scarcella 1978.
35. Hanania and Gradman 1977.
36. A. Peters (forthcoming and personal communication) points out that in some cases routines and patterns can actually influence acquisition directly by providing input to the Language Acquisition Device, just as "outside" input can. A memorized segment may contain structures that are eventually at the acquirer's i + 1. We do not know how often this occurs. Peters also points out that formulaic speech may participate in the "two-word" stage of language acquisition. This seems to happen especially under conditions of communicative stress. Performers, in such situations, consider formulaic speech utterances to be like single words or morphemes, and may juxtapose them to construct longer sentences. Researchers distinguish two forms of this. When the constituents are from pre-existing formulaic segments in the acquirer's own repertoire, it is called "build-up." Clark 1974 provides this example from first language acquisiton. Her son was heard to say *Baby Ivan have a bath,* followed by *Let's go see Baby Ivan have a bath.* The second way is "incorporation," or "coupling," in which the performer utilizes what he just heard from the input. Hatch, Peck, and Wagner-Gough 1979 provide us with this example: Adult: *Where are you going?* Child: *Where are you going is house.* For more discussion see Peters (forthcoming) and MacWhinney 1980.
37. Peters 1977.
38. Stafford and Covitt 1978.
39. See Krashen, Long, and Scarcella 1979 for a review of the research supporting these generalizations.

40. Scarcella and Higa 1981.
41. While some studies indicate a gradual decrease in ultimate attainment with age of first exposure (e.g. Oyama 1976), others report that puberty is the turning point (e.g. Seliger, Krashen, and Ladefoged 1975), with those beginning second language acquisition before age 10 being more successful than those starting after 15. Seliger et al. report that those beginning between 10 and 15 have a 50-50 chance of attaining native-like performance levels.
42. See Elkind 1967. Formal operations refers to the ability to think abstractly, to form general rules, to be able to arrive at conclusions on the basis of abstract argumentation, to relate pure ideas to each other without the necessity of referring to concrete objects, to have "ideas about ideas." The pre-formal thinker, the concrete thinker, only arrives at abstraction from direct experience with concrete objects, he has to "live through it" or experience things himself. The ability to think abstractly may be related to the ability to possess a mental representation of a language, or a conscious grammar. Thus, formal operations may be responsible for the conscious Monitor. Not everyone attains formal operations (not every second language performer is a Monitor user) and formal operations does not arrive at the same time in everyone.

Chapter Three

Implications of Second Language Acquisition Theory for the Classroom

IMPLICATIONS OF SECOND LANGUAGE
ACQUISITION THEORY

> Comprehension
> Speaking
> The Role of Grammar

THE NATURAL APPROACH: GUIDELINES

THE NATURAL APPROACH AND LANGUAGE
ACQUISITION THEORY

In the previous chapter, we outlined a theory of second language acquisition. This theory consists of a set of interrelated hypotheses that are supported by empirical data. The aim of this chapter is to present very briefly some of the general implications of these hypotheses for the second language classroom. We will then discuss how these general conclusions can be applied to form a coherent approach to second language teaching: the Natural Approach. In the following chapters, these conclusions will be discussed in some detail with specific suggestions for application in the classroom.

IMPLICATIONS OF SECOND LANGUAGE ACQUISITION THEORY

Comprehension

The most important implications derive directly from the Input Hypothesis. If it is true that we acquire languages via comprehensible input, and if language acquisition is central, not language learning, then it follows that the most important element of any language teaching program is input. According to the Input Hypothesis, language acquisition can only take place when a message which is being transmitted is understood, i.e., when the focus is on **what** is being said rather than on the form of the message. This could be referred to as the "Great Paradox of Language Teaching": **Language is best taught when it is being used to transmit messages, not when it is explicity taught for conscious learning.**

The requirement that input be comprehensible has several interesting implications for classroom practice. First, it implies that whatever helps comprehension is important. This is why visual aids are so useful. Pictures and other visuals supply for the adult what the "here and now" does for the child. They supply the extra-linguistic context that helps the acquirer to understand and thereby to acquire. Second, it implies that vocabulary is important. Grammar-based approaches to language teaching deliberately limit vocabulary in order to concentrate on syntax. We are suggesting that vocabulary should not be avoided: with more vocabulary, there will be more comprehension and with more comprehension, there will be more acquisition! This is not to say that vocabulary is sufficient; it is to say that its importance is not to be denied. A third implication is that in giving input, in talking to students, the teacher needs to be concerned primarily with whether the students understand the message. Instructors need not be overly concerned with whether they are using certain structures; the Natural Order Hypothesis does not imply that grammatical structures need to be supplied in the natural order. According to the principle of the Net (discussed with the Input Hypothesis in Chapter Two), if enough successful communication is taking place and if the students understand the message, there will be input at the $i+1$ level, the next set of structures the student is due to acquire, and acquisition will proceed.

The discussion of age differences and individual variations implies that comprehensible input will be the crucial element of a language teaching program for all students, young and old, grammar learners or not. While some second language students may be learners, everyone is an acquirer. Thus, the crucial and central component of any language teaching method is input that is understood.

Another implication is that the classroom may be a very good place for second language acquisition, especially at the beginning and intermediate levels. As Wagner-Gough and Hatch have pointed out, input to older acquirers tends to be more complex syntactically, it is not always tied to the here and now, and adults must deal with a far wider range of topics. [1] Because of this, adult beginners, even if they are in the country where the language is spoken, will not at first be able to understand much of what they hear around them. Natural input is often too complex for beginners and can be difficult to utilize for language acquisition. In the second language classroom, we can give adults a "concentrated dose" of comprehensible input, 40 or 60 minutes of useful input at one time. This can be much more efficient than relying exclusively on the informal linguistic environment. We are therefore very enthusiastic and optimistic about the potential of the classroom as a place for second language acquisition!

The Affective Filter Hypothesis along with the Input Hypothesis, implies that effective classroom input must be interesting. This is easier said than done, of course. The necessity of interesting input is founded on good theoretical reasons. We want students to be concerned with the message, not with the form, in order to bring their filters down. This means that when student interests and goals vary, there may have to be variety in the topics chosen for the classroom activities. Topics of universal appeal will be especially valuable, especially those of personal interest to the students.

Speaking

According to the Input Hypothesis, speaking is not absolutely essential for language acquisition. We acquire from what we hear (or read) and understand, not from what we say. The Input Hypothesis claims that the best way to teach speaking is to focus on listening (and reading) and spoken fluency will **emerge** on its own. For foreign language teaching, in situations where there is no vital need for early communication, we can allow speaking to emerge in its own time. For language students who are actually in the country where the language is being taught, we may be justifiably concerned with early production, and may want to "beat the system" by encouraging some limited early production, via routines and patterns. In such cases, such routines and patterns should focus on the immediate situational needs of the students. For these students, short, useful dialogs may be of great benefit. We must bear in mind, however, that teaching dialogs is not the same thing as providing input for language acquisition, but rather, it is a short-term substitute.

Speaking is of course a primary goal of most language students. It is also important in that it stimulates conversation, which in turn will encourage more comprehensible input.

The Role of Grammar

As we have discussed earlier, the study of grammar does have a role in the language program. Our goal is to produce optimal Monitor-users, performers who can use grammar as a supplement to acquisition in situations where grammar use is appropriate. But this implies that grammar instruction has a limited role. Only certain rules need be taught even for optimal Monitor use: for most learners only the late-acquired simpler rules. Also, only certain students will be able to profit from grammar instruction (recall the discussion of individual variation in Chapter Two). Finally, grammar use should be restricted to situations where it will not interfere with communication. We should not expect our students to be concerned with fine points of grammar while they are speaking in free conversation; rather, the time to use the Monitor is in writing and in prepared speech.

Finally, in certain programs, there is a place for "advanced" grammar study. There are students who are, for some reason, very interested in the study of grammar for its own sake, perhaps future linguists and language teachers. Presenting advanced structure to these students in the target language could be of some use in that it is a topic of interest. The theory implies, however, that it is the language of explanation that will help with acquisition, not the grammatical facts learned! In other words, the medium is the message. If teachers realize that complex grammar is not easily usable in real performance, and that the teacher-talk input is the most valuable part of the presentation in terms of acquisition of the target language, such grammar classes may be highly beneficial. They are, however, not for everyone, and should be, at the most, an optional part of the program.

THE NATURAL APPROACH: GUIDELINES

In this section, we illustrate how the Natural Approach is consistent with the implications of the theory of second language acquisition we have just discussed. We do not claim that the Natural Approach is the only possible way of implementing these applications. Nor do we claim that the Natural Approach is entirely new. It shares many features with older "traditional" approaches discussed in Chapter One, many of which contain features that are consistent with the results of second language acquisition summarized in Chapter Two. It is, however, a coherent approach, fairly easy to adapt to different needs, and one that has already shown its worth in actual practice.

(1) The goal of the Natural Approach is communication skills.
The general goal is the ability to communicate with native speakers of the
target language. Particular objectives are also specified in communicative
terms. For example, we expect students in beginning stages to be able to
talk about themselves and their families. The focus is primarily on the acquisition of the ability to communicate messages using the target language.
This is not to imply that we are unconcerned with grammatical accuracy.
We are concerned, but our claim is that in the long run students will speak
with more grammatical accuracy if the initial emphasis is on communication
skills, since real communication results in receiving more comprehensible
input, both in the classroom and in the outside world. Students who can
communicate with native speakers will also tend to do so after any formal
language training is completed, thus insuring futher comprehensible input
and more improvement in accuracy in their speech.

(2) Comprehension precedes production. If communicative ability is
based on acquired knowledge, then it follows that the students must first
learn to comprehend. Most of the N.A. techniques for classroom activities in
early stages are oriented to giving students comprehensible input without
requiring oral production in the target language.

(3) Production emerges. Speech (and writing) production emerges as
the acquisition process progresses. We expect speech at first to be incomplete
and, for the most part, to contain many errors. Students are not forced to
respond in the target language, and when they do start to produce, their
speech usually consists of simple words and short phrases. In cases in which
the instructor and students share a common language, some students may
prefer to use this language in early responses, or even mix the two languages. In input-rich environments in which affective filters are low, usually
this kind of mixed mode is quickly left behind.

(4) Acquisition activities are central. Since acquisition is central to
developing communication skills, the great majority of class time is devoted
to activities which provide input for acquisition. Subsequent sections in this
book will be devoted to illustrations and discussions of activities which
supply input which can be utilized by the students in the acquisition process.
On the other hand, conscious learning is important for the monitoring function for students who are able to benefit from such information and is provided as the supplementary exercises. One of the central tasks of the instructor is to present an optimal balance of acquisition and learning activities.
This balance is, of course, quite different in different contexts, depending
on factors which we have mentioned: goals of the students, age, ability to
utilize grammar in monitoring, and so forth.

(5) Lower the affective filter. Since input cannot be utilized by adults
for acquisition if the affective filter is high, the value of all classroom activities
is measured by the degree to which the affective filter is lowered, as well as
the amount of comprehensible input provided.

Natural Approach and Second Language Acquisition Theory

The five simple principles of the Natural Approach are completely consistent with the hypothesis we discussed in Chapter Two.

Acquisition-Learning Hypothesis. The basic organization of the second language course is according to the acquisition-learning distinction. Most of the classroom time is spent on activities which foster acquisition; learning exercises are important in certain cases, but always play a more peripheral role.

The Natural Order Hypothesis. By allowing student errors to occur without undue emphasis on error correction, the Natural Approach teacher allows the natural order to take its course. There is no expectation that students will perform late acquired items correctly in early stages of second language acquisition. A teacher of English as a second language, for example, will not expect full correctness for the third person singular -s for verbs (a very late acquired item) in their students' speech, nor will instructors of Romance languages expect students to apply rules of gender agreement in the noun phrase accurately and efficiently except in situations of easy monitoring.

The Monitor Hypothesis. The Natural Approach encourages appropriate and optimal Monitor use. Students are expected to use the conscious grammar when they have time, when the focus is on form, and when they know the rule. This occurs mostly in written work, in prepared speech, or on homework assignments. They are not expected to apply rules consciously in the oral communicative activities of the classroom.

The Input Hypothesis. The classroom is the source of input for the language students, a place where they can obtain the comprehensible input necessary for language acquisition. The Natural Approach is consistent with language acquisition theory in that it puts input in a central place in the curriculum.

The Affective Filter Hypothesis. Probably no method will be totally successful in eliminating the affective filter. The Natural Approach aims to bring it down to as low a level as possible by taking the student "off the defensive" [2] and lowering the anxiety level of the acquisition situation. This is done in several ways. First, the fact that there is no demand for early speech production (see Chapter Four for teaching techniques), reduces the anxiety of the students considerably, since it allows for concentration on one skill at a time. Second, students are allowed to make the decision, individually, when they wish to begin speaking the target language. When they do begin to speak, production in the form of single words or short phrases as responses is accepted in a positive manner. Thus, any sort of attempt at speaking is rewarded positively. Finally, errors of any form are not corrected directly (although in many cases the "correct" version of what the student has said will be included in the teachers' response to the student, see discussion of "expansions" in Chapter Four). We do not wish students to have an excessive concern for correctness in early stages of language acquisition since, for the most part, Monitor use simply slows down the communication process and acquisition is delayed. Finally, the requirement that the input be interesting to the students will contribute to a more relaxed classroom.

The Role of Aptitude. We have hypothesized that second language aptitude, defined as a score on a standard aptitude test (e.g. the MLAT), relates primarily to language learning and not language acquisition. The acquisition-oriented second language classroom, then, should minimize individual differences in aptitude. If all students are acquirers, and if the classroom provides input for acquisition with a low affective filter, both high and low aptitude students should acquire communication skills successfully. Aptitude differences, it is predicted, will be felt in Monitor use, for example, in written work or in the homework. Aptitude differences play a large role if grammatical accuracy is emphasized; but in the Natural Approach, in which primarily communicative skills are stressed, they play a much smaller role.

The First Language. In Chapter Two it was claimed that second language performers may "fall back" on first language grammatical competence when they have to produce "too early" in a second language. They may use the "L1 plus Monitor Mode", using the syntactic rules of the first language, vocabulary of the second, and the conscious Monitor to make necessary repairs. The Natural Approach tries to minimize the necessity for the use of this mode by not insisting on early second language use in the classroom, and by allowing students to utilize less than complete sentences. It thus allows the students to use their naturally acquired competence and does not require them to rely on less natural modes of production in early stages. It should not be thought, however, that any approach will completely eliminate this mode of production. When students try to express themselves in the target language beyond their acquired ability, they will tend to fall back on the L 1 plus Monitor Mode.

Routines and Patterns. We claimed that routines and patterns are not acquired language and that they do not become acquired language. Teaching methods that rely extensively on dialogs and pattern practice do make this assumption, however. There is essentially no emphasis on pattern practice in the Natural Approach, and pre-created dialogs play a small role. There is no assumption that true (acquired) second language competence will develop from the repetition of certain sentences and patterns. The Natural Approach, in fact, does not provide for standard repetition practice in any form.

As we mentioned earlier, routines and patterns may be helpful for encouraging input in the real world, as they may help the aquirer manage conversations. Limited dialog practice, using these useful routines and patterns, is included but is not a central part of the pedagogical program.

Individual Variation. The Natural Approach has the potential of providing for all variations in Monitor use. For example, the distribution of learning exercises and acquisition activities can be varied. In some programs under-users of the Monitor, students who have no aptitude for grammar or who
simply are not interested in grammar, will concentrate almost completely on
acquisition activities. (Let us be clear that we still expect the under-users to
improve in accuracy in their speech through acquisition.) Optimal-users will
be able to add learned grammatical competence to their acquired competence through learning exercises. The over-user is prevented from over-
emphasizing grammar: although conscious grammar may be the focus of
some learning exercises, it will not be the focus for most of the activities in the
classroom, nor will it be tested extensively. For many adult second language
acquirers, some learning exercises can be quite helpful even though, strictly
speaking, they do not contribute directly to progress in language acquisition.
As discussed in Chapter Two, t the optimal-user of the Monitor will be able to
use the Monitor to produce learned but not yet acquired rules (such as
simple morphology and agreement rules) and to thus "fill the gaps" left by
incomplete acquisition by proper use of the conscious grammar. Often
these are errors that do not impair communication but mark the speaker
as being "non-native."

Age Difference. Child-adult differences in second language acquisition
and performance can easily be dealt with by the Natural Approach. First, as
we have said, all performers, young and old, are acquirers, and the aquisi-
tion-oriented classroom will serve everyone. We will, of course, need to
consider differences in *what* is discussed and dealt with in the classroom.
Clearly, children in second language programs (ESL, FLES) will not be interested in the same topics that adult students are interested in. The principle of providing comprehensible input remains the same, however.

According to our discussion, most adult students differ from children in
that they have a greater ability to consciously learn grammar rules. (On the
other hand, they have higher affective filters.) Accordingly, the proportion of
learning exercises (aimed at building and using the Monitor) will vary according to age: for younger children almost all language skills must be acquired directly from natural language acquisition experiences. Learning exercises will be used only for older students, and then in a judicious manner
since acquisition activities are more important even in the case of adults.

Notes

1. Wagner-Gaugh and Hatch 1976.
2. Stevick 1976.

Chapter Four

Getting Started with the Natural Approach

CURRICULUM ORGANIZATION

    Goals

    Goals in a Natural Approach Class

    The Role of Grammar in Setting Goals

    General Communicative Goals

    Informing Students About Methodology

    Developing Strategies for Listening Comprehension

CLASSROOM ACTIVITIES IN EARLY STAGES

    Listening Comprehension (Prespeech) Activities

    Early Production

    Extending Production

MANAGING CLASSROOM ACTIVITIES

    Student Responses

    Student Errors in Early Stages

    Reading and Writing in Early Stages

    Pronunciation

    Expectations of the Early Stages

CURRICULUM ORGANIZATION

Goals

A decision on the methods and materials to be used in a course is possible only once the goals of that course have been defined. The purpose of a language course will vary according to the needs of the students and their particular interests. Often students must be able to use a language for some specific purpose: working in an area in which a different language is spoken, reading technical material, traveling in a foreign country, working with members of a language minority group, and so forth. The purpose of a language course may simply be pleasure: many would like to be able to speak another language not because they need to, but because they think that they will enjoy the experience.

In addition to language courses for specific purposes, there are general language courses as a part of the secondary or university curriculum. The purpose of these courses in various parts of the world is similar, but there are some notable differences. In Europe, especially in smaller countries, the study of other languages is highly valued because of their usefulness. A Dutchman, in order to do business or to travel, must use another language. In other parts of the world, on the other hand, the communicative function is not as highly valued since the language being studied is not used in normal daily activities. Such is the case in the United States and in much of Latin America. In the United States, it is not necessary to be able to communicate in another language in order to do business or travel, although both activities may be enhanced by knowledge of another language. In Latin America, there is no need to know much of languages other than Spanish or Portuguese for oral communication, although a reading knowledge of English is extremely helpful in many professions. Therefore, the relative importance given to language study and to the acquisition of various oral and writing skills will necessarily vary according to the needs of the students.

The approach in general language courses is to try to develop the "four skills" — listening comprehension, speaking, reading, and writing. There are other possible goals, however. One goal often mentioned in connection with these courses is to develop a greater cultural awareness on the part of the students. Or, others may wish to promote a more open attitude toward speakers of other languages. In some cases, instructors place a high value on the development of the students themselves — their self-images and their relationships with others.

What is most important is that the goals of the course be specified. In the following paragraphs we will try to explain how we think that goals may be defined so as to be useful to both the instructor and the student. We do not pretend that our suggestions cover all possible goals for language courses in all situations, rather we have tried to limit ourselves to those goals which seem to us to be common to most language courses in a wide variety of contexts. We will divide the goals according to basic personal communication skills and academic learning skills.[1] We list below some examples of each type:

Basic personal communication skills: oral

(1) participate in a conversation with one or more speakers of L2
(2) listen to a conversation between other speakers
(3) listen to announcements in public places
(4) request information in public places
(5) listen to radio, television, movies, music

Basic personal communication skills: written

(1) read and write notes to friends or workers
(2) read signs, including instructions
(3) read and fill out forms (applications and other documents)
(4) read advertisements (windows, newspapers, magazines)
(5) read and write personal letters
(6) pleasure reading

Academic learning skills: oral

(1) present a class report
(2) listen to a lecture
(3) listen to a movie or other audiovisual presentation with academic content
(4) listen to and participate in panel and classroom discussions

Academic learning skills: written

(1) read textbooks
(2) write reports, essays
(3) read and discuss literature
(4) study for and take an exam
(5) take notes in class

We have two reasons for focusing the language course in terms of these sorts of competencies. One is to point out that in most cases the general language course cannot possibly attempt to develop all of these skills in the target language. The second is that in formulating the goals of the course, the need of the students for these sorts of skills should be considered. For example, it is often the case that students learn how to analyze poetry in another language, but cannot read signs or instructions in that language. We are not saying that one skill is intrinsically more important than the other, only that each skill should be carefully considered, and the proposed goals of a language course should be justified in terms of usefulness and basic educational philosophy.

Goals in a Natural Approach Class

The Natural Approach is designed to develop basic personal communication skills — both oral and written. It was not developed specifically to teach academic learning skills, although it appears reasonable to assume that a good basis in the former will lead to greater success in the latter. Thus, in the remainder of this text we will concentrate primarily on basic personal communication skills with only passing reference to the teaching of academic learning skills. Please remember that in doing this we do not mean to imply that academic learning skills (the reading of literature, for example) are not important — they certainly are, but only that other methodologies, or modifications of the method presented here may be called for.

Basic personal oral communication goals may be expressed in terms of situations, functions and topics. For example, we define situations in which the students must use the target language, for example, in a hotel, the function of the interaction, in this case a request for information, and the topic of communication, e.g., obtaining lodging. In the following outline, we list topics and situations which are likely to be most useful to beginning students.

Preliminary Unit: Learning to Understand
TOPICS

1. Names
2. Description of students
3. Family
4. Numbers
5. Clothing
6. Colors
7. Objects in the classroom

SITUATIONS

1. Greetings
2. Classroom commands

I. Students in the classroom
TOPICS

1. Personal identification (name, address, telephone number, age, sex, nationality, date of birth, marital status)
2. Description of school environment (identification, description and location of people and objects in the classroom, description and location of buildings)
3. Classes
4. Telling time

II. *Recreation and leisure activities*

TOPICS

1. Favorite activities
2. Sports and games
3. Climate and seasons
4. Weather
5. Seasonal activities

6. Holiday activities
7. Parties
8. Abilities
9. Cultural and artistic interests

SITUATIONS

1. Playing games, sports

III. *Family, friends and daily activities*

TOPICS

1. Family and relatives
2. Physical states
3. Emotional states

4. Daily activities
5. Holiday and vacation activities
6. Pets

SITUATIONS

1. Introductions, meeting people   2. Visiting relatives

IV. *Plans, obligations and careers*

TOPICS

1. Immediate future plans
2. General future activities
3. Obligations
4. Hopes and desires

5. Careers and professions
6. Place of work
7. Work activities
8. Salary and money

SITUATIONS

1. Job interview   2. Talking on the job.

V. *Residence*

TOPICS

1. Place of residence
2. Rooms of a house
3. Furniture and household items

4. Activities at home
5. Household items
6. Amenities

SITUATIONS

1. Looking for a place to live
2. Moving

VI. *Narrating past experiences*

TOPICS

1. Immediate past events
2. Yesterday's activities
3. Weekend events

4. Holidays and parties
5. Trips and vacations
6. Experiences

SITUATIONS
1. Friends recounting experiences

VII. *Health, illnesses and emergencies*

TOPICS
1. Parts of the body
2. Physical states
3. Mental states and moods
4. Health maintenance
5. Health professions
6. Medicines and diseases

SITUATIONS
1. Visits to doctor
2. Hospitals
3. Health interviews
4. Buying medicines
5. Emergencies (accidents)

VIII. *Eating*

TOPICS
1. Foods
2. Beverages

SITUATIONS
1. Ordering a meal in a restaurant
2. Shopping in a supermarket
3. Preparing food from recipes

IX. *Travel and transportation*

TOPICS
1. Geography
2. Modes of transportation
3. Vacations
4. Experiences on trips
5. Languages
6. New experiences

SITUATIONS
1. Buying gasoline
2. Exchanging money
3. Clearing customs
4. Obtaining lodging
5. Buying tickets
6. Making reservations

X. *Shopping and buying*

TOPICS
1. Money and prices
2. Fashions
3. Gifts
4. Products

SITUATIONS
1. Selling and buying
2. Shopping
3. Bargaining

XI. *Youth*

TOPICS
1. Childhood experiences
2. Primary school experiences
3. Teen years experiences
4. Adult expectations and activities

SITUATIONS
1. Reminiscing with friends
2. Sharing photo albums
3. Looking at school yearbooks

XII. *Giving directions and instructions*

SITUATIONS
1. Giving orders at home
2. Giving instructions at school
3. Following maps
4. Finding locations
5. Following game instructions
6. Giving an invitation
7. Making an appointment

XIII. *Values*

TOPICS
1. Family
2. Friendship
3. Love
4. Marriage
5. Sex roles and stereotypes
6. Goals
7. Religious beliefs

XIV. *Issues and current events*

TOPICS
1. Environmental problems
2. Economic issues
3. Education
4. Employment and careers
5. Ethical issues
6. Politics
7. Crime
8. Sports
9. Social events
10. Cultural events
11. Minority groups
12. Science and health

SITUATIONS
1. Discussing last night's news broadcast
2. Discussing a recent movie

The preceding list only suggests situations and topics that students could use in oral communication with speakers of the target language. These topics are also appropriate for reading and writing activities, if these latter skills are goals in the language course. Also, for each topic and situation there are various language functions which the students will acquire: making an invitation, reacting to others' opinions, asking others to do something, asking for clarification, and so forth.

What do we expect of the students mastering these goals? We expect that they will be able to function adequately in the target situation. They will understand the speaker of the target language (perhaps with requests for clarification) and will be able to convey (in a non-insulting manner) their requests and ideas. They need not know every word in a particular semantic domain, nor is it necessary that the syntax and morphology be flawless — but their production does need to be understood. They should be able to make the meaning clear but not necessarily be accurate in all details of grammar.

The Role of Grammar in Setting Goals

The goals of a Natural Approach class are based on an assessment of student needs. We determine the situations in which they will use the target language and the sorts of topics they will have to communicate information about. In setting communication goals, we do not expect the students at the end of a particular course to have acquired a certain group of structures or forms. Instead we expect them to be able to deal with a particular set of topics in a given situation. We do not organize the activities of the class about a grammatical syllabus.

It is important to delineate clearly the relationship between grammar and communication goals. In order to communicate about a certain topic in a particular situation, there are a series of language functions which may be expressed by certain grammatical structures (including both syntax and morphology) and certain vocabulary. For example, if the students are to learn how to order meals in a restaurant, they must know some appropriate food and restaurant-related vocabulary. But in order to communicate their desires, beginning students can simply string the appropriate lexical items together in some "logical" order, even if they have not yet acquired (or learned) any syntax or morphology. [2] This strategy will in many cases be sufficient for basic communication. Thus, of the two tools for communication, vocabulary and grammar, the former is clearly the most essential one.

On the other hand, we clearly do want and expect that students will acquire grammar — we do not expect that Natural Approach students will continue to use only simple "stringing" techniques to produce speech. It is also our goal to produce efficient "Monitor users," i.e., those who can Monitor when appropriate without interfering with the flow of communication. Thus, we want to plan for both acquisition opportunities and for learning possibilities where appropriate.

In embracing a "communication" philosophy, we are not rejecting the idea that students need to acquire (and in some cases learn) a great deal of grammar. In fact, according to the theory of second language acquisition outlined in Chapter Two, our experience is that they will acquire more

grammar this way. Stated simply, focusing on communication goals provides far more comprehensible, meaningful input and encourages more language acquisition, than basing the course on grammar. If we provide discussion, hence input, over a wide variety of topics while pursuing communicative goals, the necessary grammatical structures are automatically provided in the input.

We believe that relying on a grammatical syllabus, no matter how "contextualized," would not be as efficient even if the goal were just the acquisition of syntax. As noted in Chapter Two, the grammatical syllabus assumes that we know the correct Natural Order of presentation and acquisition; we don't: what we have is information about a few structures in a few languages. The net of structure provided by communicative and comprehended input, on the other hand, will automatically provide the "next" structure, or $i+1$, even if the teacher or syllabus designer does not know precisely what that structure is.

Also, grammatical syllabi only work for those students who happen to be ready for the "structure of the day". However, all learners vary in their rate of acquisition. As some students may have had a chance to acquire some of the target language outside the class, it is highly unlikely that all students will be at exactly the same stage of development. Aiming at one grammatical structure at a time is likely to miss the mark for many, if not most, students. On the other hand, if the students understand most of what is said, $i+1$ is supplied for everyone (even though it may be a slightly different $i+1$ for different students), and language acquisition will take place.

A third problem with grammatically-based syllabi is that in nearly all cases there is no real provision for review. If students miss a structure, they nearly always have to "wait until next year"! This is not the case with natural, communicative input. A given student's $i + 1$ will be provided over and over assuming there is enough input. Finally, what may be the most serious problem with the grammatical syllabus is that a grammatical focus invariably distorts any attempt to communicate. The goal of even the most clever contextualization is teaching structure, and this seriously constrains what can be discussed or read. It thus appears to be the case that we not only don't have to use a grammatical syllabus in encouraging acquisition, it is better not to even try. [3]

The learning of syntax and morphology for the Monitor function, on the other hand, although of far less importance than acquisition in most contexts, can be provided for by a grammatical syllabus. Recall, however, that the monitoring function makes sense only after there is something to monitor, i.e., after communication strategies are somewhat developed and after the acquisition process is well established. Therefore, we defer discussion of the grammatical syllabus and the use of grammar exercises in the Natural Approach to Chapter Six, concentrating for the present on the most important aspects of the Natural Approach course — communicative activities for acquisition.

General Communicative Goals

In planning a communicative based syllabus, we use three stages as a basis for beginners; all involve personalization and the use of familiar topics and situations. The first stage is aimed primarily at lowering the affective filter by putting the students into situations in which they can get to know each other personally. We call this the **personal identification stage.** The students learn how to describe themselves, their family, and their friends in the target language. This implies learning to talk about their interests, studies, desires, future plans and daily life as well as these same topics in relation to others close them and their fellow classmates (Topics I-V, pages 67-68). These are also the same topics which the students might discuss with native speakers in real situations in first encounters.

The second stage consists of giving the students comprehensible input about **experiences** and allowing for opportunities to engage in conversations about their own experiences. Students like to talk not just about themselves, but their trips, vacations, and a wide variety of experiences, such as the happiest moment of their lives or the saddest one. They will want to recount experiences from their childhoods as well as primary and secondary school experiences. It also includes using the target language in common situations they are likely to encounter in traveling or living in a country where the target language is spoken. This stage continues the focus on lowering the affective filter. (Topics VI-XII).

The third stage we suggest for beginners consists of input and discussions, concerning **opinions.** They discuss political issues, civil rights, marriage, family, and so forth, and gain the competence to express their own views. (Topics XIII-XIV).

Within these three stages, there is ample opportunity to include a wide variety of communicative situations: a trip to the doctor, making purchases, preparing a meal, and so forth. [4] Which of these specific goals is chosen will depend on its relevance to the interests and needs of each group of students.

Informing Students about Methodology

Not only should course goals be specified, but experience tells us that whenever possible students can and should be informed as to the relationship between the goals and the particular methodology which will be used to attain these goals. There are several reasons for this. First, in language teaching our goal is not simply to teach someone "so much" Spanish or French. Our goals should also include teaching our students how foreign and second languages are acquired. We want to equip our students to use the natural environment for further language acquisition, to progress to more advanced stages in the language studied, or to acquire additional languages. Some discussion of the general principles and strategies of second language acquisition will make our students less dependent on us.[5]

Second, thanks to a long tradition of pattern drill and conscious rule teaching, some "de-briefing" is usually necessary. Teachers of English as a second language, for example, know that many students expect a diet of drill and grammar. The Natural Approach needs to be introduced and often even justified to such students.[6] Students need to be given some idea as to what they can expect to be able to do in the target language after completing a given course of study.

Correct expectations will both encourage students as well as prevent disappointment. Here is a sample of what students can be told:

*After 100-150 hours of Natural Approach Spanish, you **will** be able to: "get around" in Spanish; you will be able to communicate with a monolingual native speaker of Spanish without difficulty; read most ordinary texts in Spanish with some use of a dictionary; know enough Spanish to continue to improve on your own.*

*After 100-150 hours of Natural Approach Spanish you will **not** be able to: pass for a native speaker, use Spanish as easily as you use English, understand native speakers when they talk to each other (you will probably not be able to eavesdrop successfully); use Spanish on the telephone with great comfort; participate easily in a conversation with several other native speakers on unfamiliar topics.*

In addition, we find that it is helpful to give to the class information about how the class will be conducted, i.e., a sort of "rules of the game" which they will need to know in order to participate successfully in the initial acquisition experience. The following are suggestions:

1. *Your teacher will speak in French (for example) exclusively. You may answer in either English or in French. You are free to use English until you yourself feel ready to try speaking French. You should not try to use French until you are comfortable doing so. (This, of course, applies only to classes with a common language which the instructor understands.)*
2. *When you do try to speak in the new language, the teacher is interested in what you have to say — not whether you have said it perfectly. Neither you nor the teacher will be overly concerned with grammar errors in your speech while you are a beginner.*
3. *You do not have to use full sentences. You may talk in short phrases or even use just one word when that is appropriate.*
4. *Remember that as long as you **understand** what the teacher is saying,*

you are acquiring French. This means that you should focus on **what** *is being said, the message, rather than on* **how** *it is being said.*

Developing Strategies for Listening Comprehension

Since the main thrust of the course, especially in initial stages, will be the acquisition rather than the learning of language rules, it is absolutely essential that the student comprehend speech in the target language as quickly as possible. Very often students, especially those with previous language study experience, believe that the ability to comprehend another language develops slowly after much study of vocabulary and grammar. If this were the case, very few people would acquire languages in natural situations. It is important that students understand the process by which they will comprehend what the instructor says to them in the target language.

Most adults expect to understand a new language by learning the meaning of every word they hear. Instead they should learn to interpret general meaning without always understanding all the details. This is neither automatic nor simple for most adults. They must be told that the instructor will use words, forms and structures that they have not yet studied or discussed. However, by paying close attention to the context and the key words in the sentences, they will be able to make a good guess at the meaning of the sentence. This "contextual inferencing" is the secret to learning to understand a second language and to the eventual success of the student in the acquisition process. The students should be aware of this "inferencing" strategy, since on the first day the instructor will begin speaking in the target language, and will want them to experience immediate success in understanding. They should leave the class thinking, "I really did understand most of what was said and it wasn't so difficult." What must happen is that by hearing everything in a clear context, the student is able to follow the communication without necessarily understanding all of the language *per se*. When this goal is attained, students will believe they can understand a new language. This is an important psychological barrier which must be broken through if the students are to be successful in language acquisition.

We turn now to a discussion of actual classroom activities that can be used at different stages of student development in the Natural Approach classroom.

CLASSROOM ACTIVITIES IN EARLY STAGES

Listening Comprehension (Prespeech) Activities

Since we do not wish to force students to produce utterances in the target language until they have had an opportunity for the acquisition process to begin, the first hours of class must be devoted to activities in which the students receive comprehensible input. This means that they must be able to participate in a language activity without having to respond in the target language. There are several techniques to achieve this goal.

Particularly good is the technique developed by James Asher which forms the basis for his Total Physical Response approach. This technique consists of giving commands to students and having them actually act out what the teacher says. Since the students are not forced to produce responses in the target language, they are able to focus their entire attention on comprehension of what is said. At first the commands are quite simple: *stand up, turn around, raise your right hand.* In fact, many instructors incorporate these sorts of commands into initial language instruction. However, TPR is not limited to these simple commands.

Parts of the body as well as body actions can be taught through TPR: *lay your right hand on your head, slap your left leg, touch your right foot with your left hand, put both hands on your shoulder, first touch your nose, then stand up and turn to the right three times,* and so forth. The use of classroom props greatly expands TPR: *Pick up a pencil and put it under the book, touch a wall, go to the door and knock three times.* Any item which can be brought to class can be incorporated: *pick up the record and place it on the tray, take the green blanket to Larry, pick up the soap and take it to the woman wearing the green blouse.*

There are several other techniques which provide comprehensible input and which require as student responses only identification of students in the class. One is to use physical characteristics and clothing of the students themselves. The instructor uses context and the items themselves to make the meanings of the key words clear: *hair, brown, long, short,* etc. Then a student is described: *What is your name?* (selecting a student). *Class, look at Barbara. She has long, brown hair. Her hair is long and brown. Her hair is not short, it is long.* (Using mime, pointing and context to ensure comprehension). *What is the name of the student with long brown hair? (Barbara).* Questions such as *What is the name of the woman with short blond hair?* or *What is the name of the student sitting next to the man with short brown hair and glasses?* are very simple to understand by attending to key words, gestures and context. And they require the students only to remember and produce the name of a fellow student. In fact, in such activities the students may be only consciously focused on remembering names, and often soon "forget" they are understanding another language. (This is a good sign of a low affective filter.) The same can be done with articles of clothing and colors: *Who is wearing a yellow shirt? Who is wearing a brown dress?*

The use of visuals, especially pictures cut out from magazines, can also serve the same purpose. The instructor introduces the pictures to the entire class one at a time focusing usually on one single item or activity in the picture. He may introduce one to five new words while talking about the picture. He then passes the picture to a particular student in the class. The student's task is to remember the name of the student with a particular picture. For example, *Tom has the picture of the sailboat, Joan has the picture of the family watching television,* and so forth. The instructor will ask questions like: *Who has the picture with the sailboat? Does Susan or Tom have the picture of people on the beach?* Again, the students need only produce a name in response!

It is also possible to combine the use of pictures with Total Physical Response: *Jim, find the picture of the little girl with her dog and give it to the woman with the pink blouse.* Or, one can combine general observations about the pictures with commands: *If there is a woman in your picture, stand up. If there is something blue in your picture, touch your right shoulder.*

If the group is small, another technique is to describe several pictures, asking the students to point to the picture being described:

Picture 1. *There are several people in this picture. One appears to be a father, the other a daughter. What are they doing? Cooking. They are cooking a hamburger.*

Picture 2. *There are two men in this picture. They are young. They are boxing.*

In all these activities, the instructor attempts to maintain a constant flow of comprehensible input. The students will be successful if the instructor maintains their attention on key lexical items, uses appropriate gestures, and uses context to help them understand. If the students are literate, writing the key words on the chalkboard will give a visual image for key lexical items, and draw the students' attention to the content words.

The comprehensibility of the input will be increased if the instructor uses repetition and paraphrase: *There are two men in this picture. Two. One, two* (counting). *They are young. There are two young men. At least I think they are young. Do you think that they are young? Are the two men young? Or old? Do you think that they are young or old?* The instructor can weave these repetitions naturally into discourse so that they do not sound like repetitions. Nor is there need to pause at each potential question point for an answer, since each question is usually paraphrased in two or three ways before the instructor expects a response.

The whole point of this section is that it is relatively simple to teach comprehension without requiring more than minimal production. There are numerous advantages of a preproduction stage. The students are given the opportunity to become comfortable with the class activities, the instructor, and with classmates without being forced to respond in the target language. In addition, production of utterances in a new language is much more complex than comprehension. In order to produce an utterance, the students must recall the words they wish to use, articulate new sounds, and use as much syntax and morphology as they have acquired (and/or learned). Doing all of this requires a tremendous amount of conscious "processing time" for beginners. By concentrating on comprehension strategies only, all attention can be directed to developing comprehension skills. An equally important goal of this preproduction stage is to convince students that they will be successful in the language course. Finally, the preproduction stage allows the student an opportunity to begin the acquisition process.

We have no illusions that the sort of input in the target language and the interaction with the students described above constitute "real communication." At this stage, however, the techniques described are realistic enough to (1) provide comprehensible input, (2) maintain focus on the message and (3) help lower affective filters. Thus, we can be assured that the acquisition process will begin.

This preproduction phase with concentration on comprehension is especially important for students living in an area in which the target language is the language for daily communication in the society. In these second language contexts, the ability to comprehend speech in a wide variety of contexts takes on added importance. If the instructor concentrates on giving the students experience with comprehension of speech through vocabulary recognition, the ability of the students to understand speech outside the target language classroom can increase very rapidly. If, on the other hand, the students are required to produce (with accuracy in pronunciation and grammar) everything they hear in the input, their progress will be very slow both in the target language classroom and more importantly in their interactions with native speakers outside the classroom. [7]

Early Production

Target language production in an input-rich natural environment begins with single word utterances or short phrases. The shift from answers with gestures, names, or with *yes-no* to producing words in the target language usually comes naturally and spontaneously after several hours of input. The length of time of the preproduction period will of course vary with the amount of input provided and the rate at which and degree to which the affective filter can be lowered. Our experience is that adults make the transition from listening to production quite rapidly. Some adults begin producing single words or short phrases after one or two hours of comprehensible input. Others need up to ten or fifteen hours of input before they feel comfortable enough to produce. Adolescents often need considerable exposure to the new language before they attempt to produce utterances. This is probably due more to affective factors than to any intrinsic difficulties with language acquisition. [8] Young children very often show a delay in production from one to six months. [9]

The transition from preproduction input to a stage in which the students begin to speak is simple if opportunities for production are made available gradually within the normal comprehension (preproduction) activities. The earliest verbal responses in the target language will be *yes-no* in reply to a simple question: *Does Brian have the picture of the boy with his brother? Is the boy tall? Is he wearing blue jeans? Does Jean have the picture of the men playing golf? Is there a mountain in the picture? Is it raining? Does Jane have the picture of the woman talking on the phone? Is she beautiful? Is she wearing a blue blouse?*

The next step integrates the use of *"either-or"* questions into the comprehension questions: *Is this a dog or a cat? Is this woman tall or short? Is Mary wearing a red or a green blouse?* Acceptable answers are: *dog, tall, green.* Answering an either-or question amounts to no more than a repetition of a word which the instructor has just pronounced. Thus, although the students are actually producing target language words for the first time, the correct pronunciation and form are immediately available in the preceding input.

From either-or questions, it is an easy step (although one not necessarily taken immediately) to ask for identification of items which have been introduced several times. *What is this? What color is her skirt? What is he doing?* In all cases the students need only say a single word to answer the question. Or, the instructor may start an utterance and leave a pause. *He has on a red . . .* Most students will immediately say *shirt* (if indeed it is the shirt that is red).

These input techniques for encouraging early production do not constitute a discrete stage of language development but rather are an extension of the comprehension stage. When the instructor begins to ask questions and make comments which require single word responses, the emphasis is still on giving comprehensible input. At first, most of the questions should require only gestures or names as answers with only a few requiring single word answers. As the students become comfortable with producing responses in the target language, their use can be increased, but the goal of supplying large quantities of comprehensible input is still more important at this stage than the students' initial attempts at production.

The following is an example of **teacher-talk** based on pictures, i.e., comprehensible input, which includes examples of all of these techniques for encouraging early production.

> *Is there a woman in this picture? (Yes). Is there a man in the picture? (No). Is the woman old or young? (Young). Yes, she's young, but very ugly. (Class responds no, pretty). That's right, she's not ugly, she's pretty. What is she wearing? (Dress). Yes, she's wearing a dress. What color is the dress? (Blue). Right, she's wearing a blue dress. And what do you see behind her? (Tree). Yes, there are trees. Are they tall? (Yes). And beside her is a _____ (dog). Yes, a large dog is standing to her right.*

It is also important to continue to expand the net of comprehensible input. The net of syntax and morphology will expand naturally without any overt attention on the part of the instructor. However, new vocabulary can be deliberately introduced into this sort of input.

What do you see in this picture? (Man). Yes, there is a man. Where is he? (Beach). Yes, he is sitting on the beach. What is in front of him? (Students don't know the word). That's a sailboat. Is it large or small? (Small). Is it in the water or on the beach? (In water). Yes, it is floating (new word, use mime to explain) in the water. Can stones float? (No). Can people float? (Some). Right. If you know how to swim (new word, use mime), you can float.

Indeed, new words should be introduced and then reused many times before the students are expected to use them in their responses. Thus, at any given time the comprehensible input serves to introduce new vocabulary, reuse vocabulary which has previously been introduced, and to give an opportunity for the students to produce vocabulary which has been used by the instructor so often that it has been acquired (or in some cases learned). In this way, at the same time the students are producing words they have acquired, the input contains new words which will form part of the material to be acquired. Comprehension, in this way, always outpaces production, not just in the preproduction stage, but throughout Natural Approach activities.

The early production activities that we have suggested correspond to the "personal identification" stage, thereby allowing the instructor to concentrate on lowering the affective filter while providing input for expanding listening comprehension. Any of the first few topics listed as goals at the beginning of this chapter would be appropriate in this early stage.

To this point we have only suggested the use of visuals, mostly pictures, as a basis for oral input and single-word responses. These techniques can be used with both children and adults and with students who have no literacy skills. But if the students are at all literate in their first language, there are two other sources of stimuli for giving comprehensible input in the single-word stage: charts and advertisements.

	Natalia	Abdul	Helmut	Ito
8:30	ESL	Math	Science	Social Studies
9:45	Break	Break	Break	Break
10:00	Math	Science	ESL	ESL
11:15	Phys Ed	Art	Health	Art
12:00	Lunch	Lunch	Lunch	Lunch
1:00	French	History	ESL	ESL
1:45	Social Studies	ESL	Speech	Phys Ed

Charts collect information in an easily interpretable form. The chart above is an example of school subjects of foreign students in a secondary school in an English speaking country. Teacher talk using the chart as a basis for providing comprehensible input might run like this:

This is a chart of the schedule of classes for four students. What are the names of the students on this chart? (Natalia, Abdul, Helmut, Ito). What time is the morning break? (9:45). Right, the morning break is at nine forty-five. Do classes begin at 8:30? (Yes). Is that earlier or later than our classes begin? (Earlier). What is Abdul's first class of the morning? (Math). Does anyone in our class have Math at 8:30? (Students respond perhaps by raising their hands or by other gesture). *What class do you have?* (addressing one of the volunteers) *(Biology). Does Natalia have PhysEd or Math at 11:15? (PhysEd). Do these students have lunch at the same or different times? (Same). Yes, everyone eats lunch at ____ (twelve o'clock). Which student takes a foreign language? (Natalia). Does anyone in our class speak French?* (follow-up with appropriate response or question).

This chart can be redone using actual students in the class and their particular schedules. Most of the topics from the first section of the communicative syllabus (pp. 67-70) can be adapted in this fashion. The following are illustrations of charts from the subtopic "Students in the classroom" (p. 67)

Select three other students in your class and fill in the appropriate information. The teacher talk which will supply the comprehensible input will mainly consist of questions and comments. For example:

Let's count the number of students with blue eyes. One, two, three, four . . . Are there any others? (Jim). Oh, of course, we can't forget Jim. Yes, he has blue eyes. Now, who has brown eyes? Does Martha have brown eyes? (Yes). And what color is her hair? (Brown). Is it light brown or dark brown? (Light). Is she wearing a dress today? (No.) A skirt? (Yes). What color is the skirt? (Blue). Yes, it's a blue skirt with white stripes (new word). *Who else is wearing a skirt? (Betty). Let's try to describe it. It's _____ (green). Does it have stripes? (No). It's a solid color* (new word). *Does the blouse match?* (new word). *Look at the blouse. What color is the blouse? (Light green). Do the two greens match?* (show meaning of match).

Hair color			
brown	✔		
black			
blond			
red			

Eye color			
black			
brown	✔		
green			
blue			

Clothing			
tennis shoes	✔		
jacket	✔		
skirt			
blue jeans	✔		
sweater			
suit			
shorts			
	Mike		

Another useful activity in the early production stage is to use a form and have students interview each other to obtain the desired information. The following, for example, is a luggage tag belonging to Martha McGuire.

Identification Tag TEXAS AIRLINES

Name   *Martha McGuire*

Address *2617 Broadway Ave.*

City *Tustin*   State *Calif.*   Zip *92816*

Telephone *(714) 771-8694*

The students interview a classmate and then fill out the required information on a blank luggage tag.

In the follow-up teacher talk, the students will report on their classmates. *John, who did you interview? (Mike Evans). What is the name of the street where he lives? (Seville Way). And the city? (Lancaster). Who else in the class lives in Lancaster? (several raise hands). Let's count together, class. (Class counts with instructor). What is Mike's zip code? (78713). Does anyone else have exactly the same zip code? (two raise their hands). Does anyone have almost the same zip code? What is it? (referring to the student who raised her hand).*

Timetables are an excellent source for creating input with extensive use of numbers. The following is a flight schedule.

Los Angeles	Mexico City	Flight
lv 11:15 am	ar 3:40 pm	744
lv 6:45 pm	ar 11:10 pm	746
lv 11:40 pm	ar 4:05 am	742
Mexico City	**Los Angeles**	**Flight**
lv 8:30 am	ar 11:05 am	741
lv 3:00 pm	ar 5:30 pm	743
lv 5:00 pm	ar 7:30 pm	745

The complexity of the teacher-talk input will depend on the cognitive sophistication of the students. Adults who are used to interpreting such timetables will have no trouble with the following sorts of questions even in very early stages since the questions only require the use of numbers in the replies.

What time does flight 746 arrive in Mexico City? (11:10 pm). Does the flight leaving Los Angeles at 11:40 arrive before 7:00 the next morning? (Yes). If you need to be back in Los Angeles at 12:00 noon, what flight will you take from Mexico City? (741). How long is the flight from Mexico City to Los Angeles? (remember the time change) *(Three and one-half hours).*

Students with less experience with such cognitively demanding tasks can be given much simpler input.

What time does Flight 744 leave Los Angeles? And what time does it arrive in Mexico City? How many flights per day are there from Los Angeles to Mexico City? And how many return flights are there? If you miss the first flight of the day, how long do you have to wait until the next flight?

Simple advertisements are helpful in early stages as a basis for providing input which contains numbers used in prices. The following are sample clothing ads accompanied by possible teacher-talk input.

$16.99 Jeans	**9.97**
$24 Stretch Jeans	**16.97**
$16.99 Corduroy* Jeans	**9.97**
$20.99 Western Shirts	**13.97**
*Polyester and cotton	**thru Jan. 30**

How much are the jeans? How much do you save? Which costs more, the jeans or the corduroy jeans? How much were the Western shirts originally? If you buy one shirt and two pairs of jeans, what is the least it will cost you? Look at the ad for the sale on designer sportswear. What is the cost now of the least expensive skirt? And the most expensive skirt? What was the most expensive item mentioned in this ad? The least expensive? If you buy a skirt and a blouse, what is the most it could cost you? And the least?

Extending Production

How long the students stay in the one-word stage will vary individually. Although questions using the techniques described in the previous section do not require more than a one-word response, it is possible to expand the answer and many students do so and produce short phrases after several hours of comprehension activities.

One of the earliest models we use to encourage the development of early production is the **open-ended sentence.** Here, the students are given a prefabricated pattern, a sentence with an open slot provided for their contribution.

Very simple sentences which can result in lists of words are helpful: *In this room there is a _____. I am wearing a _____. In my purse there is a _____. In my bedroom I have a _____. After class I want to _____.* Although the student is obliged only to produce a single word creatively, many will quickly use short phrases to fill the slot.

Also useful for early production is the **open dialog.** Two and three line dialogs lend themselves to creative production even when the student is only beginning to make the transition out of the one-word stage. They may be written on the board or on an overhead projector.

— *Where are you going?*	— *Hi, my name is _____.*
— *To the _____.*	— *Pleased to meet you. I'm _____.*
— *What for?*	— *Are you from _____?*
— *To _____.*	— *Yes. (No, I'm from _____.)*

These dialogs are practiced in small groups depending on the number of participants in the activity. Since many of the later production activities involve working in small groups, this helps to prepare the class for this sort of language activity. [10]

Another useful technique in early stages is **association.** This activity provides exposure to a great deal of comprehensible vocabulary in an interesting and meaningful way. The meaning of a new item is associated not only with its target language form but with a particular student. To illustrate the model, let us consider the following example, intended to get students to participate in conversation about activities they enjoy doing.

The students are told that the goal of the activity is to learn to talk about things they like to do. This will entail learning *I like to* and *He/She likes to* as **prefabricated patterns,** that is, as memorized "chunks" that can be used as unanalyzed pieces of language in conversation and that also may serve as comprehensible input. The pattern should be written on the board and remain there throughout the activity.

> *I like to* _____
> *you like to* _____
> *he likes to* _____
> *she likes to* _____

Each student will indicate a single activity he or she enjoys: *I like to fish, to swim, to play basketball* and so forth. Each student chooses only one activity and no student may choose an activity if it has already been selected. Suppose the activity first chosen is "to eat." The instructor writes on the board *eat* while saying *Jim likes to eat.* (Students are not required to do choral repetition, but some do repeat the word, or the entire utterance at this point). Next, the instructor makes several comments or asks the student simple questions about the activity. In this case, the instructor might comment that we all like to eat, or that most of us eat too much, or anything else which the class can understand.

The instructor then asks the next student for an activity and repeats the process. After several verbs have been introduced, the instructor systematically reviews by asking questions which require only a single word answer. *Who likes to eat? Does Martin like to ski or to play volleyball? Joyce doesn't like to run, does she? Does Jim like to swim?* This conversational review during the activity has two goals: to provide more comprehensible input and to allow time for the association of new vocabulary with individual students.

In addition to these activities, all of the techniques described in the previous section can serve to extend speech. The use of pictures is the same as in the preproduction stage except that the instructor input includes questions which can be answered in short phrases or sentences. The same is true of charts and advertisements.

MANAGING CLASSROOM ACTIVITIES

Student Responses

In the early stages of speech production we use **random volunteered group responses,** which place little demand on the individual student but allow early use of the target language. The instructor asks a question and anyone and everyone can respond as they wish without raising hands. Suppose, for example, that the instructor asks about the weather: *How's the weather today?* Some students will answer internally, silently. Others will mumble a barely audible response. However, some students, perhaps half of the class, will utter responses which are both audible and comprehensible. They will probably include *fine, good, cool, cloudy,* and so forth. That is, they are all correct answers (semantically) and all are produced at approximately the same time. In cases of questions with a single logical answer, as in most of the questions from the preceding section, the responses will be the same, but somewhat dispersed in time. In initial stages practically all activities are done in this mode. The result is that the students hear a great deal of input during a single class session (usually several hundred utterances) to which they all can respond in some way.

Random volunteered group responses are not as orderly as a group choral repetition, but approximate real communication while the latter do not. Our experience is that older groups adapt themselves rapidly to this sort of response freedom. For children, it is the normal way to respond. [11]

Student Errors in Early Stages

The possibility of the students making errors in early stages is limited simply because the possibilities of oral production are also limited. During Total Physical Response (TPR) activities, the students may err only by failing to understand and by executing the command incorrectly. It is unlikely however, that the entire class will misunderstand; therefore, there will always be a correct model to imitate. In our experience with TPR, students constantly check the actions of their classmates and self correct almost immediately when necessary.

In the other activities of the prespeaking stage, the only responses which are required are the names of the other students in the class and perhaps a simple *yes* or *no*. Mistakes with these activities usually stem from a misunderstanding of the question (indicated by silence or the identification of the wrong student) or from forgetting the name of the student being described. In either case, unless the instructor has asked the question of an individual student (a rare practice in early stages), correction is automatic and immediate since, as in TPR, most of the class will have answered correctly at the same time.

Mistakes appear when the student starts to produce utterances in the target language. However, in early Natural Approach activities, errors are minimized since in the activities designed to encourage initial speech production, only single word (or short phrase) responses are normally appropriate. When they occur, errors are of three types. First, the answer given may be incorrect. For example, the instructor pointing to a picture of a table asks, *What is this?* and student replies, *chair.* In this case, the instructor is justified in correcting the error directly. *No, this isn't a chair, it's a table.*

Another possibility is that the utterance is appropriate and well-formed, but pronounced incorrectly. In this case, the instructor can simply use the mispronounced lexical item in an expanded answer. For example, instructor says, *This woman is wearing a red _____* (pointing to a blouse). A student mispronounces the word *blouse.* The instructor might reply *Yes, that's right, she's wearing a red blouse.*

Also common (and probably universal) are responses which are appropriate but syntactically incomplete or morphologically ill-formed. For example, the instructor asks, *Is this a picture of a man or a woman?* Students reply, *woman,* omitting the required article. The instructor again gives a positive response (and more comprehensible input), *Yes, this is a woman.* Or to the question, *What is the man doing in this picture?* the students may reply *run.* The instructor expands the answer, *Yes, that's right, he's running.*

The point of these expansions is to supply comprehensible input and encourage communication, not to expect that the students will correct themselves and repeat the utterance in a correct form. Furthermore, it should not be thought that the students will in all (or even in most) cases, immediately attend to and benefit from these expansions. If the student's level of acquisition is not ready for the acquisition of a particular rule, then most likely the expansion will be accepted only as a sign of comprehension and success in communication, but will not be utilized for progress in acquisition of grammar. Indeed, in many cases the rules themselves will be so complex that the student will have to hear these expansions (and other input) many times before acquisition of the particular rule or item is even begun. Thus, theoretically, expansions may not be absolutely necessary. They are probably helpful, however, in that they provide additional comprehensible input. In the activities which encourage more complex speech production, there will, of course, be more errors. The "cure" however, is the same: more comprehensible input provided by the instructor.[12]

In any case, whatever technique is followed to ensure that the student is surrounded with comprehensible input, the important point is that direct correction of errors is not necessary and will in most cases be detrimental to the objective of lowering the affective filters. We will comment further on the correction of student errors in Chapter Seven.

Reading and Writing in Early Stages

In courses in which reading and writing are not goals, the activities we have described in this chapter can be done without any reference to the printed word. With young children, this is also the case since even in the situation in which reading and writing will follow, these activities can serve as a "reading readiness" period. On the other hand, with adults (and adolescents, who will later be learning how to read and write in the target language) both reading and writing can be profitably begun during both the prespeaking and early production stages.

Initially, TPR commands are normally given only in oral form. Later, the instructor may wish to write them on the chalkboard and let the students copy them in a notebook. This is of course only a copy exercise, but it does allow for the opportunity to see in print what they already have comprehended in the spoken language. If the native language uses the same writing system or the same alphabet as the target language, this will involve only a minor adjustment of associating some new sounds to familiar symbols and perhaps a few new symbols.

With input using descriptions of class companions and pictures, many instructors using the Natural Approach report good results with a technique which includes writing new, key words on the chalkboard as they are introduced for the first time in the comprehensible input which the instructor supplies to the students. These words can be copied into notebooks by the students as they are introduced. Most instructors have reported that this technique does not, for the most part, distract from the concentration on the message of the input, since what is written are new content words, not grammatical forms (articles, function words, auxiliaries, copulas, endings and other grammatical morphemes). In addition, this often has the effect of slowing down the rate of input, thus increasing comprehension. For many students it also helps to focus on the key lexical items rather than the totality of the elements in the sentence. Finally, in our experience, many adults are quite visually oriented and this visual image of a new word helps them to retain it more quickly and longer.

On the other hand, there are dangers to supplying written input too soon. First of all, some students have reported that seeing the printed word in early stages is simply distracting. Others have reported that the practice leads them to want to produce before they have acquired enough phonology and before they have begun to make sound-letter correspondences firmly. This leads to trying to pronounce the words they have written before they are really acquired. While all of these objections are to a point valid, they can be overcome. Natural Approach instructors do not push for speech production before the students are ready and often remind them that they need not try to pronounce the words they have written until after a few hours of experience with listening comprehension.

Whether or not this particular practice of writing words on the chalk-board in early stages is used or not, we do wish to emphasize our firm disagreement with the practice in the early days of audiolingualism of not letting the students see the printed word in any form before the material is completely learned in an aural-oral mode. As noted in Chapter One, this was a very frustrating practice for both instructors and students and caused many more affectively negative feelings than could have ever been compensated for by the supposed reduction in transfer of bad pronunciation habits from the native language.

Nor should instructors worry that students who see the words which are introduced will become dependent on the printed word as is the case in many methodologies tied closely to a textbook. The students see only a few key words in each utterance and the greatest part of the input they receive is completely oral without direct reference to anything written.

We will have more to say about the teaching of reading and writing in Chapter Six.

Pronunciation

In a beginning language course, the issue of when to teach pronunciation inevitably arises. There has been surprisingly little research, however, addressing the question of whether pronunciation can even be taught or learned.

In a very recent study,[13] however, Purcell and Suter surveyed acquirers of English as a second language, and concluded that accuracy of pronunciation of English correlated with the acquirers' first language (speakers of Arabic and Farsi had better accents than speakers of Japanese and Thai), the amount of interaction with English speakers, performance on a test of phonetic ability, and the degree of concern the speakers had about their accent. Surprisingly enough, the amount of formal classroom training in ESL, even when the courses were specifically aimed at pronunciation, did not relate to pronunciation ability. Thus, it may be possible that direct classroom exercises are of limited use.

Pronunciation ability, or a good accent, may be nearly completely dependent on what has been acquired, not on rules which have been learned. It is possible to learn conscious rules about pronunciation, but performers, especially in the beginning stages, usually have too many more important things to attend to in performance.

One interesting hypothesis is that pronunciation ability, or phonological competence, is in fact acquired quite rapidly, but that speakers do not "perform" their competence possibly because they do not feel comfortable using an authentic accent in the second language. They therefore "fall back" on first language phonological competence, resulting in an "accent."[14]

If formal teaching has such a limited effect on pronunciation, then what we can do is simply provide an environment where acquisition of phonology can take place and provide an atmosphere where students can feel comfortable and where they will be more prone to perform their competence. Thus, in the Natural Approach we do not recommend any specific activities for pronunciation, especially in early stages.

The preproduction period seems to be of benefit by allowing the students to develop a "feel" for phonology before they are required to produce it. It is not clear, for example, that direct repetition by the student after the instructor, a practice often used in the audiolingual approach, actually encourages the development of pronunciation skills. There is experimental evidence that suggests, in fact, that a silent period may be of greater benefit. [15] In early Natural Approach activities, although students are not forced into choral group repetition of new words and phrases, some students do repeat and imitate the pronunciation immediately, while others simply listen (and may repeat internally).

Pronunciation can, of course, be presented for conscious learning via language lab exercises assigned as homework. These are groups of exercises with simple explanations for the correspondence of letters and sounds and guidelines for the production of these sounds. As we stated, it is not clear that such exercises actually improve the pronunciation of most students, but some students believe them to be helpful. Since such rules are learned consciously, however, they will be available only in situations in which the students can monitor their speech easily.

Many instructors are convinced that if they do not emphasize correct pronunciation at the beginning of a course, students will establish "bad" habits which will be difficult, if not impossible, to change later. While it appears to be true that one who has spoken a language for many years with a very strong accent may have difficulty changing, there is no evidence, on the other hand, that pronunciation habits are so firmly established in the first couple of years of language study; indeed, informal experiences with thousands of language students lead us to believe that pronunciation often improves with experience and can improve considerably as late as the third or fourth year of language study.

Another mistaken belief, in our opinion, is that students must achieve native-like pronunciation skills to be successful. Only language instructors set such difficult standards since native speakers never expect foreigners to speak their language without an accent. The native speaker adopts more realistic expectations: the acquirer should pronounce in a fashion which is understandable without an extraordinary effort by the native speaker. Nor should the acquirers' pronunciation be overly irritating or distracting. But these requirements are a far cry from the "perfection" demanded by many language instructors.

In summary, then, in the Natural Approach, we do not place undue emphasis in early stages on perfection in the students' pronunciation, but rather concentrate on providing a good model with large quantities of comprehensible input before production is attempted.

Expectations of the Early Stages

For us the most important goal of the early stages of the Natural Approach is to lower the affective filter. This is because a high filter will prevent acquisition — the central goal of the Natural Approach. We want students to become comfortable with the class activities and with interacting with each other in the target language. They should begin to develop confidence in their ability to comprehend the target language as well as have a positive attitude towards acquiring a new language in general.

The early activities are meant to initiate the acquisition process, to help students unconsciously adjust to new patterns of intonation, rhythm, and a new sound system. The acquisition of syntax is begun at least on the level of word order. At first students probably do little more than begin the acquisition of transformations which permute elements (as in negation or question formation), but with some experience can understand sentences using such transformations. It is doubtful if morphology is noticed (either consciously or unconsciously) since morphology in general is not necessary at first for partial comprehension and indeed acquirers in early stages usually ignore it completely. What is acquired then in this stage are general sorts of listening strategies, i.e., rules of interpretation of utterances without depending on an extensive knowledge of syntax and morphology.

On the other hand, a great deal of vocabulary must be acquired very early on, at least on a recognition level, if the student is to be successful with the Natural Approach. Indeed, many instructors who have had extensive experience teaching with Natural Approach activities characterize the early stages as consisting of activities whose purpose is to give comprehensible input with an ever expanding vocabulary.

Learning plays a very small role in Natural Approach classes in initial stages. In the case of children, all activities are directed at acquisition. For adolescents and adults, some provision for learning may be helpful although learning will not of course dominate the class. In the first place, many adults would not be happy with an approach which depends entirely on unconscious processes. They are used to studying new material on a conscious level and feel a need to "study" the language they are learning. It may be true, although we have no formal evidence, that some conscious study of vocabulary helps to speed the acquisition process since the more words the students can recognize in an utterance the more comprehensible the input will be.[16]   In some Natural Approach classes in which students study outside of class, the initial homework assignments have involved exercises to review vocabulary. (For further discussion of vocabulary, see Chapter Six.)

In addition, some adults are quite proficient in the study of grammar, and they may feel more comfortable if they can read a good succinct explanation of the forms and structures the instructor is using in the input they are receiving. In some Natural Approach courses in secondary schools and universities, the students have a grammar handbook and some students report that such materials are a great help to them.

The help from the study of grammar is probably more psychological than linguistic. It is probable that the study of grammar rules in early stages of language acquisition contributes very little directly to the ability to comprehend the input from the instructor and that its benefits are more in the area of increased security for certain kinds of students. On the other hand, our experience is that too much emphasis on grammar study can be very detrimental to the acquisition process. If the students learn a number of morphological and syntactic rules, they may spend so much mental "processing" time on these items during a comprehension activity that they "miss" some of the key lexical items and actually understand less than students who have not studied grammar. If this happens, and we have personally seen many such instances, acquisition actually falls behind. Thus, too much learning in some cases can be a detriment to overall progress in the development of communication skills.

In conclusion, the question of the integration of materials to promote learning in the initial stages of the Natural Approach becomes one of balance. Learning materials (vocabulary and grammar study) should be included if the instructor believes that the students can benefit from such study without interfering with the acquisition process.

Notes

1. We are using the terminology introduced by Cummins 1980 but now modified, Cummins 1981.
2. See e.g. Givon 1979.
3. It may be said that the Natural Approach uses a "notional" or semantic syllabus in that class activities are centered around topics or situations and not around particular structures. It is thus fundamentally in agreement with the "Communicative Approach" proposed by several scholars (see especially Wilkins, 1976). It differs from these approaches, however, in several ways. While other attempts to apply notional syllabuses focus on production exercises and error correction, the Natural Approach focuses on input. It assumes that most of the rules relating notions and functions to grammatical form (rules of communicative competence) will be acquired, not learned, and that a great deal of the grammatical structure will be acquired as well. The Natural Approach does not expect full communicative competence after one year of study. It does expect students to be able to *understand* a great deal of real language use, and thus be in a position to continue to acquire communicative competence on their own.
4. These stages could easily be adapted to a one-year college course or to a two- to three-year sequence in secondary schools.
5. We realize that often this is not possible in early stages of some second language courses due to the multilingual background of the students.
6. In these situations the emphasis must be on building trust and confidence in their instructor. For students who have had a great deal of formal instruction in the target language (but little practical experience), this can be a problem which must be resolved slowly but steadily. Restructuring and other group activities are helpful (See Chapter V and Christison and Bassano 1981).
7. For example, a child acquiring English in an English speaking country can acquire recognition vocabulary very rapidly, perhaps 15-30 new words per instruction hour. In a very short time, perhaps after 50-100 hours of concentrated input with emphasis on developing recognition vocabulary, children can begin to understand a great deal of the speech that surrounds them outside the ESL classroom. If, on the other hand, the instructor requires production of new vocabulary immediately upon presentation in the input, the rate is slowed down to perhaps 5-10 new words per hour. After 50-100 hours, the children will remain extremely limited in both comprehension and speech production. What is worse, the ability to use outside input will still be very low, and natural acquisition outside the classroom will be slowed down tremendously.
8. If students in their teens are not voluntarily producing words in the target language after fifty or so hours of comprehensible input, there may be serious affective blocks which will have to be attended to.
9. In many cases in which there is a long preproduction period, when speech production does finally begin it often develops quite rapidly and the child quickly catches up to the other children whose oral production began earlier.
10. We do not expect the patterns in the open-ended sentence to "turn into" creative language automatically (see discussion in Chapter Two). They will be useful, however, in allowing students to interact more easily inside and outside the classroom and thus gain more comprehensible input.
11. There may, of course, be individual and possibly cultural variation with respect to willingness to respond in this way.
12. Research on the efficacy of expansions has been done in first language acquisition with some studies concluding that expanding children's utterances has little or no effect on the rate of acquisition (Cazden 1965) while other studies conclude that they do help (Nelsen et al. 1973, Newport et al. 1977, Cross 1977). Our interpretation is that they help when they are interpreted by the acquirer as comprehensible input.
13. Purcell and Suter 1980.
14. See discussion of first language influence in Chapter Two.
15. Neufeld 1979.
16. This does not mean that we recommend studying lists of words with no opportunity to hear these words used in a communicative context — this sort of practice is undoubtedly an inefficient way of acquiring new vocabulary.

Chapter Five

Oral Communication Development Through Acquisition Activities

AFFECTIVE-HUMANISTIC ACTIVITIES

> Dialogs
> Interviews
> Preference Ranking
> Personal Charts and Tables
> Revealing Information about Yourself
> Activities Using the Imagination

PROBLEM-SOLVING ACTIVITIES

> Tasks and Series
> Charts, Graphs and Maps
> Developing Speech for Particular Situations
> Advertisements

GAMES

CONTENT ACTIVITIES

GROUPING TECHNIQUES FOR ACQUISITION ACTIVITIES

> Restructuring
> One-Centered
> Unified Group
> Dyads
> Small Groups
> Large Groups

The core of the Natural Approach classroom is a series of **acquisition activities.** By activity we mean a broad range of events which have a purpose other than conscious grammar practice. Thus, we refer to activities as opposed to audiolingual drills or cognitive learning exercises. For acquisition to take place, the topics used in each activity must be intrinsically interesting or meaningful so that the students' attention is focused on the content of the utterances instead of the form. It is also through acquisition activities that the instructor will (1) introduce new vocabulary, (2) provide the comprehensible input the students will utilize for acquisition, (3) create opportunities for student oral production, and (4) instill a sense of group belonging and cohesion which will contribute to lower affective filters.

In the early stages, as described in Chapter Four, the most important function of the activities is to provide comprehensible input, and indeed in a sense, the main task is to develop listening skills. Output in the target language is necessarily limited (usually to single words or short phrases) and plays only a minor role in furthering the acquisition process. In the "speech emerges" stage of this Chapter, however, oral production plays a more important role. In the first place, we wish to give the students ample opportunity to actualize their acquired competence: it is affectively satisfying to most students when they realize that their ability to express themselves in the target language is increasing. Secondly, as the students are able to generate more and more of the target language, this production (interlanguage) serves as comprehensible input for the other students in the class. Indeed, in this section, in many of the activities which we will describe, the student talks a great deal.

As we mentioned in Chapter Two, it is an open question whether this sort of "interlanguage talk" is helpful or harmful (or, what is more likely, both) for language acquisition. We know of no empirical studies which have investigated this question directly. However, our experience is that interlanguage does a great deal more good than harm, as long as it is not the only input the students are exposed to. It is comprehensible, it is communicative, and in many cases, for many students it contains examples of $i + 1$. These advantages, in our opinion, will outweigh the problems which might be caused by errors in the input. [1]

Each activity focuses on a particular topic and/or situation, i.e., what students in the class did last night, how to order food in a restaurant, how to apologize, how to refuse a request, what they ate for breakfast, what they like to watch on television, and so forth. The students will normally be aware of this focus. The activity may also often (but not always) have a specific form or structure which will tend to be used repeatedly in that particular activity. The purpose of the activity, however, is to supply comprehensible input, not to teach a specific structure. Most students, in fact, will probably not realize what the grammatical content of any given activity is. This is probably to their advantage, since conscious concentration on structure and form may prevent focusing on the message and may thus impede acquisition. [2]

One of the major points of Chapter Two is that comprehensible input stimulates natural language acquisition. In order for input to serve as a basis for the acquisition process, we must insure that there is:

(1) a focus on transmission of relevant information and

(2) a means of facilitating comprehension

It is quite possible, for example, to provide utterances which have some semantic content, but which do not communicate anything of importance. Suppose an instructor says, *Roger is going to the store to buy a loaf of bread.* Such a sentence carries meaning, but it may not communicate anything unless we know who Roger is and are concerned about his trip and its purpose. If the instructor merely wishes to use such a sentence as an example of the progressive tense in English, the utterance will be of little value as input for language acquisition (although it could be a part of a learning exercise or drill). To draw students' attention away from the linguistic form of an utterance, we need to go beyond a simple meaning and focus on transmission of relevant information. This requirement implies that what is talked about needs to be truly interesting. Discussing topics that are of interest to the students is not just a frill; it is essential if language acquisition is to take place. No matter how "meaningful" we try to make grammar exercises, by their very nature they will not qualify as optimal input for language acquisition since they are not being used for real communication.

A second way to help insure optimal input for language acquisition is to provide means for aiding comprehension. As we discussed earlier, caretakers help children's comprehension by limiting the topic to the "here and now." This provides extra-linguistic support and gives children an idea of what adults are talking about, allowing them to understand language that is a little beyond their current level of competence. Similarly, the language instructor can provide second language acquirers, children or adults, with extra-linguistic support. As we mentioned in Chapter Three and exemplified in Chapter Four, this is one of the reasons for the use of pictures and other realia. Good visuals are more than an interesting adjunct; they are an integral part of the equipment needed to encourage language acquisition, especially at the beginning level.

In addition to visuals, extra-linguistic information can also be used to help comprehension. The topic discussed should be somewhat familiar to the students and they should use their knowledge of the world to help them understand. If students have a general idea of what the instructor is talking about, this will help them guess at meaning. For this reason, the instructor should limit initial discussion to topics which are familiar to all students, such as where the students live, what they generally do each day, and other known landmarks and events. See, for example, the suggested communicative syllabus in Chapter Four. Instructors who discuss totally unfamiliar topics, people, or places, place a huge burden on the student trying to cope with comprehending messages in a new language.

The students also have an active role to play in insuring comprehensible input: when the listeners do not understand, they need to know how to regulate the input. Every language has ways of asking for clarification, asking speakers to repeat, to slow down, to explain. If such tools of communication are taught early, students will have some means of managing their own input. An added advantage of being able to use these aspects of conversational competence is that they help make it possible to converse with speakers of the target language outside the classroom.

It is also important that the difficulty level of the content of the activity be properly adjusted. If students encounter too much new vocabulary and structure in an activity, they tend to spend their time translating instead of participating in conversation. In terms of the theory, it is the instructor's job to make sure that the language of the activity is not far beyond the students' current level ($i + 1$).

Finally, the instructor must have some idea as to whether the students understand what is being discussed. It is not necessary to check whether every sentence is understood, nor is it necessary that every sentence be understood. In fact, it would be highly undesirable, as constant checking for comprehension would certainly get in the way of the information exchange that is at the core of the N.A. A variety of techniques to check comprehension are possible, ranging from directly asking the students whether they understand to merely noting whether their verbal and nonverbal responses indicate comprehension. Clearly the more involved the students are in the activity, the easier it will be to ascertain whether they understand the instructor's and each other's input. [3]

The effectiveness of any acquisition activity can be measured by the interest it evokes in the students to comment on or ask questions about the topics which have been treated. In fact, this spin-off in the form of additional interaction is the most valuable aspect of these activities since real communication normally takes place in these 'follow-ups.'

We will describe the acquisition activities in four groups: (1) affective-humanistic, (2) problem solving, (3) games, and (4) content. This division is principally for ease of exposition since in reality many of the activities contain elements of more than one type. For example, an affective activity may be turned into a game, or a game may involve a problem-solving activity, and so forth. All activities are designed to further the acquisition process. As such they must provide comprehensible input in two ways: through student interlanguage and from the teacher-talk included in the activity as well as in the "follow-up" to the activity. In all cases there is a focus on content, i.e., there is a reason for doing the activity other than just language practice.

Language will, of course, be used in the activity, but language is not the conscious focus of the activity.

AFFECTIVE-HUMANISTIC ACTIVITIES

Affective activities attempt to involve students' feelings, opinions, desires, reactions, ideas and experiences. Although not all affective-humanistic activities 'work' in all situations with all students and with all instructors, they are varied enough to be of especially high value in the Natural Approach classroom. In addition, and more importantly, they meet the requirements of an acquisition activity: the focus is on content, i.e., what the students are saying, and the instructor makes a strong attempt to lower affective filters. [4]

Dialogs

We mentioned in Chapter Four the use of open dialogs to give the students the means to produce somewhat beyond their acquired capacity in early production stages. These dialogs, normally short and interesting, contain a number of routines and patterns which can be easily assimilated. The open dialogs in addition allow the student some measure of creativity.

> Student 1: Are you hungry?
> Student 2: _____
> Student 1: I think I'll order a _____ . How about you?
> Student 2: I'd prefer _____ .
>
> Student 1: Buenos días. ¿Cómo estás?
> Student 2: ¿_____ , y tú?
> Student 1: _____ .
>
> Student 1: Où est-ce que tu vas?
> Student 2: _____ .
> Student 1: Veux-tu aller avec moi _____?
> Student 2: _____ .

Often the interchanges are created to insure repeated opportunities to focus on particular conversational situations. In the following interaction the students talk about weekend activities. [5]

> Student 1: What do you like to do on Saturdays?
> Student 2: I like to _____ .
> Student 1: Did you _____ last Saturday?
> Student 2: Yes, I did.
>   (No, I didn't. I _____ .)

Thus, with the help of guidelines, the student can often begin to use structures which have not been fully acquired, and still maintain communicative interaction and creativity.

These dialogs need not be as rigid as these examples might suggest As the students advance, the guidelines can allow more room for expansion and other changes as the following interchange suggests.[6]

> Student 1: Guess what, _____ ?
> Student 2: I'm sorry, what did you say you did?
> Student 1: _____ .
> Student 2: Oh, really? When? (Where? Why? How long?)
> Student 1: _____ .

Finally, as the ability to participate in conversational exchange improves, we suggest the use of situational stimuli for the creation of original dialogs in a role-play situation. The students are divided into pairs for the following "original dialog".

> *You are a young girl who is sixteen years old. You went out with a friend at eight o'clock. You are aware of the fact that your parents require you to be at home at 11:00 at the latest. But you return at 12:30 and your father is very angry.*
>
> > *Your father: Well, I'm waiting for an explanation. Why did you return so late?*
>
> You: _____
>
> (Continue)

In suggesting the use of dialogs, we must be clear on how they are to be used. They are not, of course, the center of the program, as they are in audiolingual teaching. Dialogs should be short and should contain material that is useful in conversation. Their function is to smooth the conversation by helping students to sound more natural and more fluent with commonly discussed topics and to help them regulate input and manage conversations.

Mastery of dialogs thus has little to do directly with the acquisition process. They do, however, help beginning and intermediate students interact in conversations. This ability is especially important for students of a second language since they face immediate conversational demands outside of class. In addition, the instructor can follow up on the conversations the students have created by discussing what went on in the dialog and soliciting the students' reactions. This interchange can produce a great deal of comprehensible input.

Interviews

Students are divided into pairs and are given a series of questions to ask their partner. In early stages, the interview can be given in matrix form (on the chalkboard, overhead projector, or reproduced), so that the students are required only to supply a single word or short phrase.

> *What's your name? My name is _____ .*
> *Where do you live? I live in _____ .*
> *Do you study or work? I _____ .*

The best interviews are those which focus on interesting events in the students' own lives, for example, a series of questions about childhood:

> *When you were a child, did you have a nickname? What games did you play? When during childhood did you first notice the difference between boys and girls? What is something you once saw that gave you a scare?*

Another possibility for interviews is to choose the role of a famous person; the two participants create both questions and answers.

Interviews in the Natural Approach normally have a clear situational or topical focus. In the following interview, the focus is childhood illnesses:

> *What illnesses did you have as a child? Who took care of you? Did you have to stay in bed for long periods of time? Were you often sick as a child? What is the most serious illness you ever had?*

Interviews can be constructed around a particular grammatical structure. For example, in the following interview the questions all make use of past tense verbs.

> *Did you go to the beach a lot last summer? What did you do at night? Did you often go to the movies with friends? Did you work? Where did you live?*

If the conversational exchange is interesting enough, the grammatical focus will probably not interfere with the interaction and the activity will be successful in giving an opportunity for conversational interaction. However, a bit of restructuring with a semantic and contextual emphasis will shift the focus away from grammatical form.

> *Did you go to the beach last summer? Who with? Which beach did you go to? What did you do there? Why do you like the beach?*
>
> *What did you do at night? Did you often stay home? Did you go to the movies often? What was your favorite activity on weekend nights?*
>
> *Where did you live? With your parents? With your family? With friends? Did you like the place where you lived?*
>
> *Did you work last summer? Where? What did you do there? Did you like what you did? What did you like best about working?*

The difference between the two is clear: the first uses the interview technique as an excuse for practicing certain verb forms. The second serves as an opportunity to allow the students to talk to each other about past experiences. In the follow up with the instructor, the students will have ample comprehensible input as well as multiple opportunities to express themselves in the target language.

Interviews which focus on the students themselves, their wants, needs, feelings, opinions are the most successful. They allow for frequent interaction on a one-to-one basis. This interaction has at least two beneficial aspects: the students get to know each other in a more personal way, lowering, hopefully, affective filters, and they are given many more opportunities to express themselves in a low anxiety situation in the target language than if all activities were instructor-centered.

Thus, interviews are helpful to the acquisition process in several ways: they lower affective filters, they provide meaningful interaction in the target language, they allow for opportunities to use routines and patterns, which, as we have noted, help acquisition indirectly. Finally, they provide comprehensible input: student interlanguage during the interview and teacher-talk in the follow-up.

Preference Ranking

This activity is conducted orally but the material must be printed and distributed to the students. It consists of a simple lead-in statement followed by three or four possible responses. Students must rank (1-2-3-4) the responses according to their own preference.

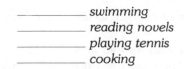

My favorite summer activity is:

_____ swimming
_____ reading novels
_____ playing tennis
_____ cooking

The point of preference ranking, of course, is not the initial ranking itself, but the follow-up conversation between the instructor and the students. It is in this follow-up that the students will receive teacher-talk input (and some student interlanguage) as well as have the opportunity to express their opinions and feelings in the target language. The following is a possible example of teacher-talk follow-up to the above preference ranking:

Who ranked swimming as number one? (Mark raises his hand). *Where do you swim, Mark? How often? When did you first learn to swim? Have you ever swum competitively? Who else in the class swims a great deal?* (Betty raises her hand). *Did you mark swimming as your first preference? Why not? What did you mark? (playing tennis). Why do you like tennis more than swimming?*

Personal Charts and Tables

The use of charts and tables was introduced in Chapter Four as a means of providing comprehensible input while requiring only one-word or short answers. But they can also be used at more advanced levels. Their role in providing input is the same, but the questions in the input can be more open, allowing the students opportunities for more complex responses.

The construction of tables of information about the students in a particular class, for example, can serve as a basis for interesting discussions. In the following example, the instructor has begun to create a chart of the weekly routines of the class members on the chalkboard.

	Monday	Wednesday	Saturday
John	works	studies	plays baseball
Jim	studies	has baseball practice	works in supermarket
Louise	studies	has swim team practice	plays waterpolo
Herman	works at record store	lifts weights	visits friends

After the chart is completed it can serve as a basis for lively questions and discussions which provide the desired comprehensible input. The level of the discussion depends on the level of the class. For students only beginning the "speech emerges" stage, the following questions would be appropriate:

> *Who has baseball practice on Wednesdays? What does John do on Saturdays? Does Herman lift weights on Wednesdays?*

As the students' ability to produce increases, so does the difficulty level of the instructor's input.

> *Does Jim have baseball practice on Wednesdays? What team is he on? What position does he play? Who plays water polo on Saturdays? Why does she play on Saturdays? Does she ever play during the week? Does she play for fun only or is she on a team? What position does she play? Do girls and women ordinarily play water polo? Why? Why not? Do you suppose Louise knows how to swim? Well? Why?*

Charts may also be created so that the students first fill out the chart with personal information and then this information serves as a basis for the class follow-up discussion. In the following chart for a beginning Spanish course, the students are asked to say whether or not they did certain activities yesterday, and if so at what time of the day. The activities include: Did you wash your car? Did you go to the beach? Did you watch television? Did you clean house? and so forth.

	Actividad	Sí/no	Hora
1.	Lavó su carro?		
2.	Fue a la playa?		
3.	Miró la televisión?		
4.	Limpió su casa?		
5.	Fue de compras?		
6.	Leyó el periódico?		
7.	Fue a una fiesta?		
8.	Vió a su novio(a)?		

In the follow-up, the instructor will extend the conversation as naturally as possible. For example,

Did you wash your car? Did you go to the beach? Did you watch television? Did you clean house? and so forth.

Another technique used in charts is to ask the students' opinion about some issue. In the following table, the students are asked to consider each activity in relation to health — is the activity good, bad, or irrelevant to good health?

Commandments for Health

1. Take a bath daily.
2. Eat vegetables frequently.
3. Lie in the sun.
4. Do exercises.
5. Drink a glass of wine daily.
6. Smoke cigarettes.
7. Drink 10 cups of coffee daily.
8. See a doctor regularly.
9. Keep your house clean.
10. Don't spend much money.

Students examine the commandments, make notes and then participate in a follow-up in which they must justify their answers. The follow-up can be done in small groups or with the class as a whole — it might be wholly student directed or controlled by the instructor depending on the proficiency of the students.

Revealing Information about Yourself

Many activities involve simply supplying personal information as a basis for discussions (as in the chart activities of the previous sections) or stating opinions about some issue or topic. In the following example, the students have to match beverages and occasions.

Occasions	Beverages
(1) breakfast	(a) soft drinks
(2) lunch	(b) coffee
(3) dinner	(c) tea
(4) before going to bed	(d) iced tea
(5) at a party	(e) mixed drinks
(6) on a picnic	(f) beer
(7) to celebrate	(g) fruit juice
(8) after playing football	(h) milk shake
(9) after swimming	(i) lemonade
(10) to stay awake	(j) milk
	(k) water

In the follow-up, teacher talk will supply comprehensible input:

What do you drink for breakfast? (coffee). How many drink coffee? Why is coffee such a popular drink in the morning? In which countries is coffee not used? What is a popular substitute for coffee? Are there some religions which do not use coffee? What is the name of the stimulant in coffee? What are other popular breakfast drinks? (juices). What are your favorite juices?

In a similar activity, the students use adverbs of frequency to describe their eating habits.

How frequently do you eat the following foods? Use (1) a lot (2) sometimes (3) almost never (4) never for your answers.

1. For breakfast I eat:	2. For lunch I eat:
a. eggs	a. a sandwich
b. ham	b. spaghetti
c. cereal	c. fried potatoes
d. hamburgers	d. a salad
e. beans	e. fried chicken
f. bananas	f. pancakes

The follow-up teacher-talk is similar to the previous activity on beverages:

Who eats eggs for breakfast? How do you cook your eggs? Does anyone like soft boiled eggs? Who eats meat in the morning? What kind? Why are certain meats preferred for breakfast? Why not? Does anyone eat hamburgers for breakfast? Why? Why not? Bananas?

The following activity combines several techniques. It is a problem solving activity in which the students cooperate in a small group to create a chart.

You and your friends decide to put together a pot luck meal. Each one of you will bring something different. Decide who will bring what and fill out the following table.

Name   Food

_____   _____

_____   _____

_____   _____

In the follow-up, the instuctor will want to find out who is bringing what and why they decided to bring that particular dish. Maybe some of the students will volunteer to explain one of their favorite recipes.

Activities Using the Imagination

There are various sorts of experiences in which the students are asked to imagine some situation, some person, or some interaction which might take place. After a period, they are asked to describe to the class what they "saw" and "said".

One common technique is to ask that students close their eyes and imagine a place with certain characteristics, for example, a pleasant place or a frightening place. After they have finished their visualizations, they voluntarily describe what they imagined either to the class as a whole or in small groups.

Visualizations serve as a basis for comprehensible input in two ways. First, the instructor may choose to guide the visualizations explicitly (appropriate pauses are not marked):

Think of a pleasant place. It may be outdoors or indoors. Look around you. Notice as much as you can. Try to feel the air around you. What is the weather like? Can you see the sun? Is it cloudy? Is it warm? Cold? Is it a calm day or are there storms on the horizon? Perhaps it is raining. Now get up and walk around your environment. What is the first thing you see? Look at it carefully. Describe it in your mind. Is it large? What is the shape? Are there colors? Is this thing you see alive? What is it doing?

Another common activity is to imagine some hypothetical situation and ask the students to relate what went on in the situation. For example, the instructor might ask the student to speak with Napoleon and give him advice in his campaign against Russia. Or, the student might interview his great, great grandmother as she crossed the plains in a covered wagon on the way to California.

In these sorts of activities, the students usually are divided into groups for the initial part of the activity and then the instructor does the follow-up with the class as a whole. In this initial stage, the students receive a good deal of interlanguage input and have ample opportunities to express themselves using their imagination. In the follow-up, the instructor has the opportunity to give comprehensible input in the form of questions, comments, and reactions.

In some activities the students may be asked to role play. A favorite topic is a group of people marooned on a desert island. Or, another group may be the first explorers on another planet describing by television what they encounter on the new planet.

The important point with activities using the imagination is that the students be interested in each other's experiences and that the focus be maintained on the topics which arise. It is the instructor who in the follow-ups to these activities must continue to provide good comprehensible input.

PROBLEM-SOLVING ACTIVITIES

The primary characteristic of these sorts of activities is that the students' attention is focused on finding a correct answer to a question, a problem or a situation. Language is used to present the problem and solve it, but language is not the overt goal of the activity. These sorts of activities are only successful if the students find them interesting, either because they are useful in some way or simply because they are an enjoyable activity. In many cases, they can be personalized; often they can be transformed into a game.

Comprehensible input in problem-solving activities is supplied in several ways. Often, the instructor gives comprehensible input in explaining the problems to be solved. In many cases, the students work on a problem in small groups using the target language to discuss and solve the problem or find the desired information. This produces, of course, interlanguage input. In other cases, the class and instructor discuss the problem together and solve it together, providing ample opportunities for both sorts of input: teacher-talk and student interlanguage.

Tasks and Series

In the tasks model, the instructor or students choose a specific activity. The object is to describe all the components of the activity. Suppose, for example, the topic is "washing a car." There will be three stages in the activity. In the initial stage the instructor will guide the students in developing the vocabulary necessary to talk about the activity. Then, together the class and instructor create utterances to describe the sequence of events to complete the activity. For example, in the above activity the class might say, *First I look for a bucket and a sponge or some rags. Then I park the car in the driveway. I use the hose to wash the car first with water only.* These utterances are developed slowly with interspersed discussion. *Which is bet-*

ter to use, a sponge or a clean rag? Should you use soap or other cleaners (such as detergents) to wash a car? During the final stage after the sequence is constructed, the discussion will broaden to include questions and discussion concerning the specific activity in the students' own lives. *How often do you wash your car? When? Where? Do you enjoy it? Why? Why not?*

If possible, students can actually do the task, which turns this into a TPR lesson. Consider the following example. [7]

GOOD MORNING

1. It's seven o'clock in the morning.
2. Wake up.
3. Stretch and yawn and rub your eyes.
4. Get up.
5. Do your exercises.
6. Go to the bathroom.
7. Wash your face.
8. Go back to your bedroom.
9. Get dressed.
10. Make the bed.
11. Go to the kitchen.
12. Eat breakfast.
13. Read the newspaper.
14. Go to the bathroom and brush your teeth.
15. Put on your coat.
16. Kiss your family goodbye.
17. Leave the house.

For this activity, the instructor brings to class as many props as possible. In this case, a minimum amount of items would include a washcloth, a toothbrush, a newspaper, and an overcoat. In preliminary conversation, the instructor talks about the props and introduces the students to the context of the series. Step two is an initial demonstration of the series in which the instructor repeats the sentences one by one demonstrating the action described by each sentence. This may require several presentations if a number of new words is involved. The third step involves the class. As the instructor again repeats the series the students must all act out the activity being described. If desired, the students read and copy the list of sentences. The instructor can answer any questions and clear up doubts that remain about the meaning of specific words or phrases. Finally, the students work in pairs and give each other these same commands (perhaps in random sequence, if they like).

One useful technique for stimulating student narration as well as providing input is the "series". This consists of a series of photographs or drawings which make a story. The students create the story using the language at their particular level. In the following example, the normal reaction is to narrate the story using past tense. But there are other possibilities. The instructor may ask the students to imagine that this is what is going to happen, or to give their reaction to each event.

Comprehensible input in a series activity can be supplied by the teacher-talk which may precede students' creation of the story and/or accompany it:

What is this young woman doing in picture one? (waking up). Where is she? What time of day shall we say it is? Do you want to give her a name? How old is she? What does she do in picture two? What does she do in picture three? Why? etc.

Charts, Graphs and Maps

Newspapers, magazines, and brochures in the target language can be excellent sources of tables, charts, diagrams, maps and so forth. These contain information which can be utilized to create communicative situations quite easily since in all cases the student will be involved in searching out information. Thus, message focus is automatically maintained. If interest in the task is created, the activity can be successful in providing input.

In the following chart of bus fares from a timetable, the students have only to match locations with fares.[8]

FARES:	LA Int'l. Airport		John Wayne/ O.C.Apt.		Long Beach Mun. Airport		Ontario Int'l Airport	
	ADULT	CHILD	ADULT	CHILD	ADULT	CHILD	ADULT	CHILD
Anaheim.	$5.20	$2.60	$2.20	$1.10	$2.60	$1.30	$5.30	$2.65
Buena Park	5.20	2.60	2.60	1.30	—	—	—	—
Fullerton	5.20	2.60	—	—	—	—	5.30*	2.65*
Long Beach Airport	4.20	2.10	3.55	1.80	—	—	6.95*	3.50*
Seal Beach	4.80	2.40	3.05	1.55	.90	.45	6.95*	3.50*
Orange	5.95	3.00	1.50	.75	—	—	—	—
Santa Ana	5.95	3.00	.90	.45	—	—	6.05*	3.05*
John Wayne Airport (Orange Co. Apt.)	6.95	3.50	—	—	3.55	1.80	6.95	3.50
Newport Beach	7.55	3.80	.90	.45	—	—	7.60*	3.80*
El Toro	7.30*	3.65*	—	—	—	—	—	—
Laguna Hills/ Mission Viejo	8.75	4.40	1.75	.90	—	—	8.75*	4.40*

This sort of chart is easily adapted to various levels. In the early production stages, questions directed at fares *(How much does it cost to travel from Seal Beach to the Long Beach Airport?)* require that the students understand the question, but they only produce numbers in their responses. As comprehension abilities increase, the same sort of table can be the basis of more complex questions *(Which is more expensive, to travel from Newport Beach to Los Angeles International Airport or to travel from Santa Ana to Ontario International Airport? If you could take a flight from either John Wayne Orange County Airport or from Los Angeles International Airport, and you were living in Buena Park, which would you prefer? What factors other than price would enter into your decision?).*

The following example of a table contains information about trips which various students took: [9]

NAME	PLACE	TRANSPOR- TATION	TIME THERE	SPENDING MONEY (U.S. dollars)	MONEY SPENT (U.S. dollars)
Bob Draper	San Francisco	train	3 weeks	$ 300	$ 200
Gino Leone	Naples	plane	1 month	800	700
Ann Gronberg	Mexico	plane	10 days	600	500
Kate Irwin	Paris	plane	2 weeks	500	400
Mike Young	Vermont	bus	6 days	100	90
The Thompsons	New York	plane	2 weeks	1,000	1,000
Sue Martin	California	train	1 week	200	100

After some work with these two activities, it will be a simple matter to construct a similar table using students in the class and recent trips they have made. The follow-up discussion then can go in the direction the class interests lie as we suggested in the previous section.

Maps can be used in the same way as charts, tables and graphs. In the following map, locating various buildings will allow practice in asking, giving, and finding directions. In the case of beginners with limited production, the map can be used in conjunction with an open-ended dialog, as in this case: [10]

A: Can I help you?
B: Where's the _____?
A: It's on _____.

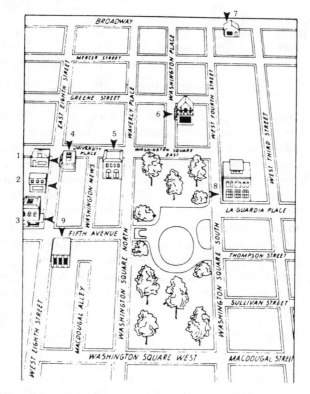

1. Brentano's Bookstore 2. Washington Square Drugstore 3. The Art Movie Theater 4. The University Coffee Shop
5. The American Language Institute 6. The University Bookstore 7. The Village Bookstore 8. The University Library
9. The Chase Manhattan Bank

Even more profitable, of course, are copies of real maps of cities which the students could possibly visit. Especially valuable are the so-called "tourist maps" in which the places of interest are identified or pictured.

In the following map activity, students work in pairs with two complementary maps and two complementary sets of instructions. The students with Map A follow the instructions in "A" and the students with Map "B" follow the instructions in Map "B". The student with Map "A" guides the student with Map "B" to the locations that are marked on Map A but not on Map B and vice versa. These sorts of activities give the students an opportunity to produce a great deal of the target language and to receive comprehensible input in the form of interlanguage talk.[11]

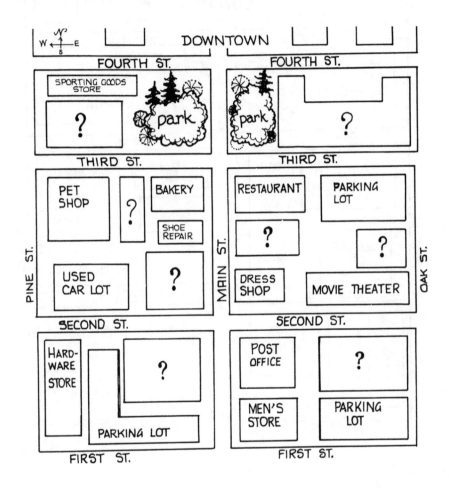

Instructions

You and your partner have different maps. *Do not look at your partner's map.* Ask your partner how to get to the places listed below, starting each time from the lower right-hand corner, where it says "Start here each time". Write the name in the right place. Then let your partner ask you.

The places you want to find are:

the hospital	the garage	the supermarket
the hi-fi shop	the department store	the nursery
the drugstore	the bank	

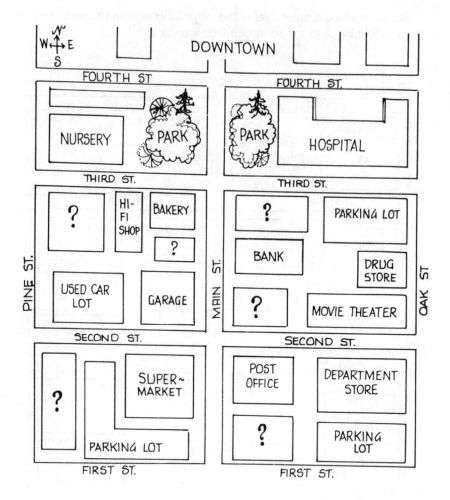

Instructions

You and your partner have different maps. *Do not look at your partner's map.* Ask your partner how to get to the places listed below, starting each time from the lower right-hand corner, where it says "Start here each time". Write the name in the right place. Then let your partner ask you.

The places you want to find are:

The sporting goods store[5]   the dress shop   the hardware store
the men's store   the restaurant   the shoe repair shop
                                   the pet shop

Developing Speech for Particular Situations

One of the goals of the Natural Approach is to prepare the student to use the target language in specific situations. In the "early" speech stage, we suggested the use of open dialogs and open-ended sentences. Both of these techniques are also valuable in encouraging speech production in particular situations. Suppose, for example, the situational focus is making essential purchases. The following is an example of an open dialog one might use in a post office.

> *Student 1 (clerk): May I help you?*
> *Student 2 (customer): Yes, I'd like _____ please.*
> *Student 1: Here you are. That will be _____ .*
> (amount)
> *Student 2: _____*

The open-ended sentence will work the same except that the instructor must supply a context. For example, the instructor might propose that the students will be spending the weekend in the mountains. They will be allowed to bring only four things with them in addition to clothing and food. The questions will be: *What will you bring?* The matrix sentence is:

> *I will bring _____ .*

A technique for somewhat more advanced students consists of creating a situation and then asking the students to supply a complete response. The following is an example of such an activity written for a unit on "restaurants and foods".

1. *You are in a restaurant full of people. You approach the hostess and you say to her "_____".*
2. *You are eating out with your parents in a restaurant. All of a sudden you discover a dead insect in your soup. You call the waiter over and you say to him "_____".*
3. *You know that your friend is on a diet and is very self-conscious of his/her weight. The waitress asks if you want some dessert. You interrupt quickly and say "_____".*
4. *You enter a new restaurant very late and find that it is completely full. The hostess asks you if you have reservations. You say: "_____".*

The descriptions of the situations themselves constitute comprehensible input, but in addition there will be ample opportunity for more teacher-talk and student interlanguage in the follow-up to the activity in which the students discuss the various responses, justifying their responses and commenting on them. These are also good occasions for discussing cultural differences, discussions which may also serve as comprehensible input.

Note that the activities described in this section are not to be done as "communicative competence" exercises — we do not demand or expect full accuracy in appropriateness, just as we do not expect it in grammar. As we noted earlier (see footnote 3, Chapter Four), the rules for communicative competence, or appropriateness, are complex and only partially described by scholars. We expect such rules to be acquired after substantial interaction with native speakers. The goal of these activities is to prepare students to participate in certain real-life situations with some efficiency, so that they can gain the input that will eventually make their performance more error-free.

This approach does not preclude the possibility of directly teaching certain aspects of appropriateness and politeness that are simple to learn and important for smooth communication. These can be done as short routines and dialogs. Subtler distinctions, such as the difference between *May I help you?* and *Could I be of assistance?* or *At your service!* will wait for acquisition.

The situational dialog which we previously discussed, in which the students actually create a dialog and role-play, is the most usual technique for acquiring situational speech skills, but of course students must be fairly well advanced in speech production for it to function well. Another possibility for students who are producing a fair amount is the situation reaction. The instructor sets up the situation and solicits students' reactions. The following are three examples of possible situations:

1. *Your washing machine is broken. You called the repair service two days ago and they made an appointment with you for today at 11 am. You have waited all morning and no one has shown up. What will you do?*

2. *You just met a young woman at the school bookstore. You exchanged telephone numbers and you promised to call at 6 this evening. You call, but her roommate tells you that she has left and left no message. What is your reaction?*

3. *You are at the bank. The teller is in the middle of taking care of you when she is called away by her superior. Fifteen minutes later you are still waiting. What should you do?*

In a variant of this model, the students are divided into groups of three or four. Each group is given a hypothetical situation. The group has to decide how it would react in that particular situation and to justify its reaction to the class. Other groups will probably react differently. The class can then speculate on reasons for different reactions. For example, *You are ten years old. Today you have an exam in your math class which you have not really studied for. What can you do so your mother will let you stay home?*

Advertisements

Newspapers or magazine advertisements are an excellent source of topics for discussions. As noted in Chapter Four, they can be adapted to either early or intermediate production stages. In the following ad,[12] for example, questions for students in early production stages would concentrate on prices and other information involving numbers. *How much does a twin-size bedspread cost? What is the telephone number of the Fox Hills Mall store?* For students whose speech is more advanced, the questions should be personalized. *Do you use a bedspread? Describe it. Do you make your bed every day? Why? Why not?* and so forth.

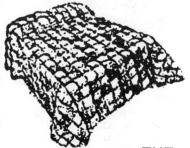
As comprehension and production increase, the difficulty level of the ads can be increased. In the following ad,[13] there are ample opportunities for the students to practice guessing at the meaning of new words or expressions from context (*carry-on, garment bag, foam padded carrier, etc.*). Questions might include: *What is the advantage of a concealed identification area? Why do some have wheels while others do not? What is the meaning of carry-on?* And of course personalization: *Who owns a complete set of luggage? Where did you buy it? Have you used it often? If I*

wanted to buy new luggage, where could you recommend that I go for good quality? Which is more important, quality or price?

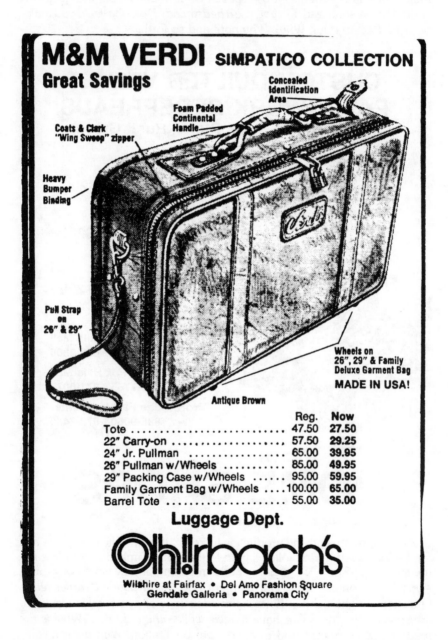

Ads can also be used to focus on certain common situations. For example, in the following ad in Spanish,[14] the instructor could focus on areas and rooms of a house. Factual questions about various houses for sale in the ad would be followed up by questions about the students' places of residence.

en guadeloupe
Ce Coin de France
au Charme Pittoresque,

un Hôtel Sympathique, en bord de mer,

le salako ★★★ nn

120 chambres climatisées
avec radio, téléphone, balcon,
2 restaurants, 2 bars, salons, salle de réunion et conférence,
piscine d'eau douce 20 m x 10 m
sur la plage: pizzeria,
une cuisine agréable et la possibilité d'échange-repas,
avec l'Auberge de la Vieille Tour,
et l'Hôtel Callinago,
Situés sur le même front de mer,
et réunis sous la même administration.

Consultez votre agent de Voyage,
il vous conseillera
ou écrivez-nous,

Hôtel Salako
BP. 8 · 97190 Gosier, Antilles Françaises
Tél 84.14.90 Télex 029 835 GL · Cable SALAKOTEL

Mr.

Adresse

Désire recevoir une documentation sur le Salako, pour
séjour ☐   séminaire ☐   groupe ☐

antilles...le soleil toute l'année

Often ads can be used simply as a lead into the particular situation the instructor and the class wish to talk about. For example, in the above ad [15] the questions would deal with the particular accommodations available in this hotel. The discussion then could range from descriptions of the sorts of hotels the students would like to stay in, to those they have actually visited. Or, one could use this ad as a starting point for a discussion of the French Antilles.

GAMES

Language instructors have always made use of games in language classrooms, mostly as a mechanism for stimulating interest and often as a reward for working diligently on other presumably less entertaining portions of the course. Our position is that games can serve very well as the basis for an acquisition activity and are therefore not a reward nor a "frill", but an important experience in the acquisition process. In this section it is not our purpose to describe a large number of games, since these are readily available from commercial publishers, but rather to show how they can be used to give comprehensible input.

Games qualify as an acquisition activity since they can be used to give comprehensible input. Students are normally interested in the outcome of the game, and in most cases the focus of attention is on the game itself and not the language forms used to play the game.[16] Indeed, experienced instructors who work with children know that they become more involved more quickly with an activity if it is presented in a game format. This is why games are indispensable in the primary school curriculum and are used, for example, extensively in ESL classes for children. Adults, on the other hand, even when they enjoy games, often do not take them seriously as valuable language experiences. This happens when instructors have failed to integrate them sufficiently into the regular class activities and have instead used them as "relaxers" and rewards.

Games can take many forms and there are many different sorts of elements which make up a game activity. We will discuss only a few of these in order to show how games function as acquisition activities. In any particular game we may focus primarily (but not exclusively) on: words, discussion, action, contest, problem solving, and guessing. Of course, most games exhibit a combination of these elements.

It is simple in many games to focus on particular words. One common technique is to make up illogical combinations and ask the students (in teams, if desired) to figure out what is wrong with the combination. For example,

> *What is strange about:*
>
> | | |
> |---|---|
> | *a bird swimming* | *a television laughing* |
> | *a table eating* | *a person flying* |
> | *a tree crying* | |

In such games it is easy to provide comprehensible input in the discussion:

Has anyone ever seen a bird swimming? (I have). What kinds of birds swim? (penguins). Has everyone seen a penguin? Do you know what a penguin is? (a black and white bird). Where do penguins live? (where it's cold). That's right, they prefer cold climates. Can penguins fly? (no, they walk and swim). Are they good at walking? Can they walk fast? (no). They're clumsy (new word).

Other games focus mostly on discussion. In one such game each student has a word or a description written on a sign taped to their backs, which others can see but they cannot. They may ask any question they want of the other students or the other students may try to give them clues to help them figure out what is written on the sign. In this case, the comprehensible input is student interlanguage.

Action games are excellent with children, but even good for most adults. A simple action game for adults is to give them a list of descriptions and ask them to find a person to match the description. For example,

Find someone who:

1. *likes to work in his/her garden*
2. *has never seen snow*
3. *is going to visit France this summer*

The students get up and mingle in the classroom asking each other questions until they find someone who fits the description. Once again, the input is student interlanguage talk.

Almost any activity can be made into a contest. Races against the clock with teams can be organized for almost any activity discussed in the previous sections. Traditional contests can also be fun and at the same time provide input. Highly useful, for example, are shows based on television games. In one such game three students are chosen for a panel. The moderator relates the outline of an experience which one of them has had (comprehensible input). All pretend to be this person. It is the task of the class to figure out who is lying. For example, the moderator might announce that one of the panelists spent three weeks in Paris when he/she was ten years old. The students then ask questions about that experience trying to see who is lying. The rules are that the one who actually had the experience must tell the truth at all times, but the others may say whatever they wish. During the question and answer section the students receive comprehensible input in the form of student interlanguage, but after the session the instructor can recap what happened, why it was difficult (or easy) to ascertain the impostors, etc. The opportunities for extensive input are numerous. Other successful adaptations of American televison game shows are: Concentration, Password, the 20,000 Pyramid and Charades.

Most games have an element of problem solving. The problem-solving activities in the preceding section, for the most part, are adaptable as games. There are basically two types of problem-solving activities: those which depend on student verbal interaction (interlanguage input) and those which can be carried out individually with no verbal production necessary. In the latter case, the important part is the instructor follow-up to give the necessary comprehensible input. Very popular with most students are problem-solving "situations". They are presented with a situation and have to figure out an answer. For example, one student is sent from the room and will be a "criminal". The class chooses a "crime" that the student has committed. The student returns and must find out what the crime was and as many details as possible. The comprehensible input can be from student interlanguage and instructor input.

An example of "silent" problem solving are mazes: the students have to find their way out of the maze. In the follow-up they must describe how to leave the maze. The instructor takes advantage of the focus on escape in order to give more input:

> *What's the first turn? (to the right). What would happen if you turned instead to the left? (you would end up at the house) Isn't there a way out of the house from the back? (no). So we continue straight ahead. For how far?*

Many games involve an element of guessing. Guessing games such as the well-known children's game "Twenty Questions" have been adapted to the language classroom in many forms. In its simplest form, a student is selected to be a particular famous person. The other students must ask questions which this student can respond to with *yes* or *no*. It is helpful when the students first play this game to give them specific suggestions for ways of asking relevant questions (*Are you a man? Are you dead? Did you die more than 100 years ago? Were you associated with politics?* etc.). An extension of this game consists of letting the students be anything they wish: a thing, an activity, a quality, and so forth. For example, if the student chooses to "be" an activity, bicycling, for example, the questions might be: *Do you do this activity in the evening? Do you do this activity for fun? Is this something everyone likes to do?* In this game the principal source of input is the students' interlanguage.

CONTENT ACTIVITIES

By 'content', we mean any activity in which the purpose is to learn something new other than language. In language instruction, this has traditionally meant learning academic subject matter such as math, science, social studies, art, and music in the target language. As in all other acquisition activities, the important characteristics are maintaining student interest and ensuring comprehensible input.

Examples of content activities include slide shows, panels, individual reports and presentations, 'show and tell' activities, music, films, film strips, television reports, news broadcasts, guest lectures, native speaker visitors, readings and discussions about any part of the target language and culture.

These activities are used in all language classes, to be sure; however, their role in the Natural Approach classroom is somewhat different. First of all, as in the case of games, they are not just pleasurable activities used as rewards for struggles with the study of grammar. Secondly, they are always presented in the target language. And finally, they may be used earlier than in most approaches since in a Natural Approach classroom, beginners are not required to produce complete error-free sentences.

The efficacy of using content activities to teach subject matter such as mathematics, science, and history in the target language has been demonstrated in immersion programs in Canada and in the United States. In these immersion programs, children are exposed to the second language via subject matter classes and acquire impressive amounts of the second language as well as the subject matter. We believe that immersion "works" for the same reason Natural Approach "works" — it provides comprehensible input in a situation in which the students' attention is on the message and not the form.[17]

GROUPING TECHNIQUES FOR ACQUISITION ACTIVITIES

Comprehensible input is the most important element in language acquisition. In beginning stages, the instructor devotes must of the time to providing this input directly to the students. As the acquisition process develops, although we still wish to continue providing comprehensible input, the instructor must also provide for activities in which the student has the opportunity to produce the target language. Although we do not believe that production per se results in more acquisition (or in better acquisition), it is important since speech will lead to more responses from the instructor and the other students. In fact, as the students progress, much input can come from the other students in the class.

The disadvantage of student production of course is that it takes a great deal of time. If each student only talks five minutes, only 12 students will be able to speak in a single class hour. For this and other reasons, we do many of the activities we have described in this chapter in smaller groups. Only in this way will more students have the opportunity to produce a sizeable amount of the target language in a single class hour.

There are many ways to divide the class for small group activities. Christison and Bassano have developed activities based on a taxonomy of student grouping activities which we consider to be very helpful.[18] They describe six sorts of grouping techniques. We will briefly describe each with an example of the sorts of acquisition activities appropriate for each grouping strategy. The strategies are: (1) restructuring, (2) one-centered, (3) unified group, (4) dyads, (5) small groups and (6) large groups.

Restructuring

Restructuring activities require the students to move about the classroom and interact with each other. They are particularly good in beginning stages and with classes in which the students do not yet know one another. They provide for maximum physical movement and interaction with minimum threat. The level of language use can be minimal in some restructuring activities.

Example: Line-ups. Students are asked to line up according to a predetermined criterion. They will usually have to speak to each other to determine the relative ordering. Possibilities.:

    (1) alphabetical according to last names
    (2) the time you went to bed last night
    (3) length of hair
    (4) the amount of money you have in your pocket right now.

One-Centered

One-centered activities are concentrated on a single volunteer but involve the entire class. This individual may be required to use a great deal of language or only respond minimally. They can be used to give a highly verbal student the attention required or to give the shy student a chance to perform successfully.

Example: A single student thinks of something which happened to him or her yesterday. The other students have to ask questions until they can guess what the event was. Suggestions: think of a positive thing which happened, an accident, a visit, a trip, something you ate, someone who called you, etc.

Unified Group

All members of the group participate in a unified group activity. The groups may be any size and there may be several in the classroom. The main characteristic is that every member of the group must participate for the activity to be successful.

Example: Make up a story with the number of lines equal to the number of students in a particular group. (For more than a single group you can use the same story and convert this activity into a timed game.) Type or write each sentence on a single slip of paper. The students each draw at random one of the slips of paper. They memorize the line and return the paper to the instructor. At a given signal, the group tries to reconstruct the story by putting the lines in order. The first group which is successful tells the story, line by line, person by person, to the rest of the class.

Dyads

Dyad activities involve the students working in pairs and are probably the most common of the Natural Approach activities for intermediate and advanced beginners. Dyads allow for more sincere interpersonal communication between the participants and give each student more opportunities for speech in a given class hour.

Example: Each pair of students must have a game board of squares; a grid of four by six squares is probably a good size. Each student is then given a set of small cards to fit the squares, each with a sketch or picture on it. The two sets are identical. The first student arranges the cards on the grid in any fashion. Then this student must give directions to the other student for placing the second set of cards in identical fashion. After the directions are complete, the students match grids to see how accurate the directions were. If the students do not know the name of an object on the cards, they may explain or describe the object, but they should not use native language equivalents.

Small Groups

Small groups are useful in many Natural Approach activities. Many instructors prefer to do almost all acquisition activities first in small groups (especially problem-solving and information gathering activities) before doing them with the class as a whole.

Example: Give each group a set of twenty pictures. The purpose is to group the pictures together according to something they have in common. You may want to specify how many different groupings the students should attempt. Each group should justify their choices.

Large Groups

These activities usually involve larger groups (7-15) or the class as a whole.

Example: Have the students in the class bring a single small object which is in some way identified with themselves. Put all of the objects in a grab bag. Then, have a student select a single item. The members of the class should try to guess to whom the item belongs. The guess should be accompanied by a reason or justification.

We have not tried to be exhaustive in listing the possibilities for the creation of acquisition activities in this chapter. Rather, the above sections are meant to be examples of the sorts of activities which we believe lend themselves easily as a basis of acquisition in the classroom, that is, they can provide comprehensible input, focus the student on messages (meaning) and contribute to a lowering of the affective filter. There are numerous other possibilities detailed in the professional literature. These include the use of music, television, radio, slides, skits, shows, games of all sorts, and a wide variety of realia which focus the student on the activity itself rather than the form of the language used to participate in the activity. Effective instructors have always made use of these sources of input, but they were usually used too sparingly, since they were believed to be of more value as entertainment than for "serious" language study. Our claim is that the opposite position is closer to the truth — language can be acquired best by involving the students in activities in which the focus and attention of the student is on the message being transmitted during the activity.

Notes

1. Krashen 1981, presents some evidence that suggests that exposure to "interlanguage talk", the speech of other language acquirers, may be useful, particularly at early stages of language acquisition.

2. Learning, of course, also has a place in the Natural Approach. However, since its role in language performance is limited (essentially to the Monitor function), we will concentrate in this chapter on activities which promote acquisition. We will return to the role of learning in Chapter Six.

3. This point cannot be overemphasized. If the instructor is unaware of the comprehension levels of the students, the input can become much too complex; the result is non-comprehension and no acquisition.

4. For numerous suggestions for affective activities, see particularly, Christenson 1977, Galyean 1976, Moskowitz 1978, Winn-Bell Olsen 1977, and Christison and Bassano 1980. Only some of the activities we will suggest are our own creation. Also, keep in mind that these are offered as examples of what might go on in a Natural Approach classroom.

5. This example is reprinted from Yorkey, R. et. al. 1978. p. 277.

6. Ibid, p. 425.

7. This example is reprinted from Romijn and Seely, p. 14.

8. This is a fare schedule from Airport Service, Inc., Anaheim, California.

9. From Yorkey, R. et. al., 1978. p. 425.

10. From Castro, O. et al. Book 1, p. 155.

11. From Winn-Bell Olsen, 1977, pp. 39-46.

12. From the Los Angeles Times.

13. Ibid.

14. From La Opinion (Los Angeles)

15. From L'Express (France).

16. It is possible to play games which do focus on particular structures or forms. For example, one can play "Bingo" in which the squares are verb forms (or some other grammatical point). The student-instructor interchange which accompanies the game can still provide good input for acquisition, while the content of the game is learning practice.

17. Immersion classes are linguistically "segregated," that is, only second language students are grouped together and no native speakers are included in such classes. This helps to insure the comprehensibility of the input since instructors cannot gauge their speech to the native speakers and leave the second language acquirers behind. See e.g., Cohen and Swain 1976. For further discussion of the use of subject matter teaching in more advanced levels, see Krashen 1982a.

18. Christison and Bassano, 1981.

Chapter Six

Additional Sources of Input for Acquisition and Learning

THE PLACE OF READING IN THE NATURAL APPROACH

Reading as Comprehensible Input

HOW SHOULD READING BE TAUGHT?

Appropriate Texts
Goals and Reading Skills
Reading Strategies
The Development of Reading Strategies without
Direct Instruction

A NON-INTERVENTIONIST READING PROGRAM

Choosing Reading Materials
Goals

INTERVENTION

A Philosophy of Intervention
Evidence for Intervention

TEACHING FOR MONITOR USE

Grammar Explanation
Learning Exercises
The Balance Between Acquisition Activities and
Learning Exercises
What Can be Monitored?

WRITING

TELEVISION AND RADIO AS INPUT SOURCES

HOMEWORK

VOCABULARY

THE PLACE OF READING IN THE NATURAL APPROACH

The Natural Approach is designed primarily to enable a beginning student to reach acceptable levels of oral communicative ability in the language classroom. Reading is a skill which is not necessary to the approach. We will suggest, however, that reading can play an important role in many Natural Approach classrooms. Reading can serve as an important source of comprehensible input and may make a significant contribution to the development of overall proficiency.

Reading as Comprehensible Input

The Input Hypothesis does not, at this time, distinguish between aural and written input. In other words, reading may also be a source of comprehensible input and may contribute significantly to competence in a second language. There is good reason, in fact, to hypothesize that reading makes a contribution to overall competence, to all four skills and not just to written performance. Clearly, written input alone will not result in spoken fluency, due to the phonological factor as well as differences in spoken and written language. Comprehensible input gained in reading, however, may contribute to a general language competence that underlies both spoken and written performance.[1]

The Natural Approach allows reading to begin as soon as the students know enough of the second language to derive meaning from the text. It does not subscribe to the once popular listening - speaking - reading - writing sequence, but instead is based on the more general input before output sequence, where input may be written as well as spoken (Chapter Three). This hypothesis predicts that reading will indeed help acquisition if it is comprehensible, read with a focus on the message, and contains $i + 1$, the acquirer's next structure or set of structures.

HOW SHOULD READING BE TAUGHT?

Do reading skills need to be taught? If so, what sort of instruction is necessary? There is a wide range of pedagogical options that currently exist in reading instruction, ranging from reading programs that do very little in the way of deliberate instruction to those that can be described as "interventionist", programs that attempt to teach many aspects of the reading skill directly. Unfortunately, little empirical research exists to help us decide which approach is correct. Our view, presented later in this section, is that some readers do not require intervention, while others require quite a bit. In our experience most students will profit by some reading instruction. In the sections that follow, we will describe the reading process as it exists and develops in the reader who needs no explicit instruction. We will then hypothesize possible points of intervention, aspects of the reading process that may be deliberately taught to advantage.

For the "natural reader", the reader who will develop reading skills without explicit instruction, we may hypothesize that all that is needed for "learning to read" is appropriate texts and some goal, that is, some reason for reading. In other words:

Text + Goal → Reading Comprehension → Language Acquisition

We examine each of these elements in turn.

Appropriate Texts

A text is appropriate for a reader if it meets two criteria. First, it must be at an appropriate level of complexity. Second, the reader has to find it interesting. Complexity in a text can have several sources, and we briefly consider three of them here:

(1) Vocabulary. Too many unfamiliar words in a passage can render it incomprehensible. What is not easy to determine is the number of unknown lexical items that can be tolerated in a reading passage. Certainly, the extremes are easy to identify: if students must translate word for word, spending most of their time with a bilingual dictionary, then the number of unknown words is too high. On the other hand, the reader need not know every word to succeed in extracting meaning. Grittner[2] gives a revealing example. In the following sentence, only a single word is presumably unknown:

> Suddenly the *flangel* swooped out of the sky and snatched an unsuspecting spider monkey from the midst of his companions.

In this case, even though we do not know the meaning of *flangel*, it is relatively easy to infer a number of attributes: it flies (swooped out of the sky), it preys on other animals (snatched a spider monkey), it is relatively large (it must fly with a monkey in its claws), and so forth. In the following sentence, however, our ability for interpretation is reduced to almost nothing:

> Suddenly the flangel *gleeped* out of the *simmel* and snatched an unsuspecting *brill* from the midst of his *fribbeling* companions.

As Grittner points out, "this sort of nonsense unit is precisely what confronts the student who is prematurely thrust into the reading of literary selections."[3] And of course what results is simply a strategy of looking up every word that the student does not understand.

If vocabulary were the only source of difficulty for readers, it would prove to be relatively simple to ascertain the "upper limit" for the introduction of new words in a passage. Since this is not the case, the number of new lexical items which can be tolerated will be dependent on the interaction of this and other sources of difficulty.

(2) Syntax. It is not easy to determine how much unfamiliar syntax can be tolerated before it interferes with the comprehension of the message. It is certainly the case that long sentences, especially with embedded clauses, will be more difficult to process.[4] Syntactic complexity, however, is not the only factor in reading difficulty. Moreover, research indicates that readers can understand passages that contain syntactic structures that are "over their heads", or well beyond their i+l. Schlesinger, in a series of studies probing reading in the first language, found that in reading passages with very complex syntax, readers use a semantic strategy to understand the text rather than a syntactic one; they may by-pass difficult structures and make hypotheses about meaning primarily based on the words used in the text.[5]

Research with second language acquirers is consistent with this conclusion: syntax makes a contribution to reading difficulty, but lexical and semantic factors can outweigh syntactic factors. Ulijn and Kempen[6], for example, in a study involving Dutch speakers acquiring French, reported that readability of a text was largely influenced by the reader's familiarity with the topic and lexical knowledge, with syntax playing a significant role only when readers faced a text on an unfamiliar topic.

This research suggests that second language [7] acquirers with limited syntactic competence can still extract meaning from texts that contain syntax that is "beyond them". They can ignore grammar that is beyond their $i+1$ and derive meaning from other sources (lexicon, grammar they have acquired, context). Readers may ignore particles, auxiliaries, and late-acquired morphology and still understand a passage if the topic is familiar and enough of the vocabulary is understood. As Hatch puts it: "If we can identify content words and if we use our knowledge of the real world, we can make fairly successful guesses about what we read without always paying attention to syntax."[8] In other words, in reading, as in aural comprehension [9], acquirers are able to tolerate some "noise" in the input data. They can comprehend a text that contains some structure beyond their $i+1$, and can thus utilize such a text for language acquisition.

(3) Semantics. Semantic difficulty can arise from several sources. One source is the degree of familiarity readers have with the topic. Passages on familiar topics will certainly be more comprehensible and hence more useful for second language acquisition than totally unfamiliar material.[10] Ideally, the reader should have texts on somewhat familiar topics that have new information so that interest is maintained.

Semantic difficulty may also arise from the inherent complexity of the topic discussed in the text. A discussion of economics, for example, will usually be more demanding than a description of a trip to the wine country of France. Appropriate texts for teaching reading and encouraging second language acquisition are not so cognitively demanding that the complexity of the topic interferes with comprehension. On the other hand, the topic has to hold the reader's interest, our next concern in this discussion.

It has been widely observed informally that if readers are genuinely interested in content, this interest can outweigh other factors to a large extent. In fact, interest in content may be the most important consideration in selecting appropriate texts. It may also be the most difficult requirement to satisfy, far more difficult than controlling for syntax or vocabulary. According to the theory of language acquisition presented in this volume, our goal is to involve students so deeply in the message that they actually "forget" it is encoded in another language.[11]

At the conclusion of this section, we will make some recommendations for selecting texts that meet these requirements, texts that students will find of interest and that are, at the same time, at the appropriate level of complexity.

Goals and Reading Skills

In addition to an interesting text at the appropriate level of difficulty, the reader also needs to have a goal; there needs to be some reason for reading, some information or message in the text that the reader is looking for.

Different goals require different kinds of reading skills. Most important to understand is the fact that we do not always read for complete comprehension.[12] We usually read for main ideas (and not necessarily all the ideas in a text), especially those ideas we can relate to our personal experience, feelings, or opinions in some way. When we read the news in the morning paper, for example, we often scan a story for certain facts we are interested in. Or we will skim quickly to get the gist of an article. These sorts of reading skills are also used in academic situations. We often skim an article or a book to see if the contents merit further attention. Certainly, when we read for pleasure in our first language we make no attempt to completely and accurately understand everything we read.

We can distinguish at least four types of reading skills. **Scanning** is making a quick overview of a passage, looking for specific information. Scanning commonly occurs when using the telephone book, reading the classified ads, ordering from a menu, and so forth. **Skimming** uses the same approach, except that instead of concentrating on specific information, we are looking for the main idea or the general gist of a passage. In pleasure reading, we usually neither skim nor scan, but read for main ideas, without always paying close attention to details. This sort of reading is termed **extensive reading,** i.e., rapid reading for main ideas of a large amount of text. **Intensive reading** is reading for complete understanding of an entire text. A student reading a problem in a chemistry text cannot be satisfied with knowing approximately what is asked. Nor will a person filling out a job application want to guess at what information is requested.

Reading Strategies

Goodman's characterization of the first language reading process[13] is widely accepted: the fluent reader does not examine every word in a linear fashion, but rather samples various linguistic cues (graphic, syntactic, and semantic), and uses knowledge of the world to arrive at a hypothesis about the meaning of the text. The reader then tests this hypothesis in various ways (reading on, re-reading). Good readers, in other words, use many sources of information.[14]

Each of the four skills described in the previous section utilizes this fundamental reading strategy to a different degree. In scanning, for example, very little of the text may be actually read. The reader approaches the text looking for specific information and utilizes cues to direct him just to the data of concern. In skimming for the general drift of a text, readers tend to rely on headings, titles, pictures, first and last sentences of paragraphs, etc., rather than examining every word. Even in extensive reading, competent readers do not examine every detail of the printed page. Goodman points out[15] that such a process would be quite inefficient and would actually detract from comprehension. Intensive reading, of course, makes maximum use of the printed text.

Some readers, we hypothesize, develop the strategies appropriate to each of the four skills through practice, and, after sufficient experience in reading for meaning, will apply the right skill at the right time. Figure One represents these cases.

FIGURE ONE [16]
A model of the reading process without direct instruction

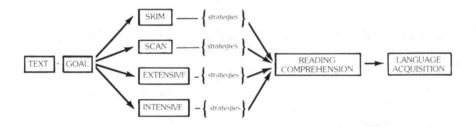

The Development of Reading Strategies without Direct Instruction

There is evidence that the reading process, as modelled in Figure One, can and does emerge, in at least some cases, without direct instruction. We briefly present the evidence for this hypothesis. Following this, we will discuss the characteristics of a reading program for such cases. The finding that direct instruction may not be necessary in some cases does not remove the need for a reading program; we can still help these natural readers a great deal.

Studies supporting the hypothesis that reading skills can "emerge" report greater use of reading strategies with greater proficiency. While more advanced second language performers can be expected to read better in the second language than beginners, due to their greater competence in syntax and vocabulary, Cziko (1978) confirmed that more advanced second language students also take more advantage of overall context and are less dependent on "local" cues to meaning.[17]

Research also indicates that in general second language readers are more dependent on local cues in the text than are readers in the first language, a result that is consistent with the idea that efficient strategies develop with experience. Hatch, Polin and Hart[18] present interesting evidence of this sort. They compared native speakers of English with acquirers of English as a second language in a simple task: crossing out the letter "e" in a printed English text. While native speakers tended to miss many "e's", especially those in function words and unstressed syllables, ESL students marked them everywhere! This result is consistent with the hypothesis that second language acquirers attend to more detail (often irrelevant!) than do native speakers.

Cohen, Glasman, Rosenbaum-Cohen, Ferrara and Fine come to similar conclusions from a different direction. In their study, they asked native speakers of English and ESL acquirers to read a history passage and answer questions probing detail as well as questions requiring some generalizing from the text. They reported several instances in which native speakers erred but ESL acquirers did not. Such cases "generally were a result of the non-natives' more 'local' reading. The natives tended to pass over specific details which they mistakenly considered unimportant. The non-natives assigned all material equal value, which in these cases produced the correct answer, since the questions concerned detail."[19]

A NON-INTERVENTIONIST READING PROGRAM

Readers who do not require deliberate instruction in developing reading strategies will still profit from a reading program. Following Figure One, such a program will consist of two parts:

(1) appropriate texts
(2) appropriate goals

When these two elements are provided, the rest will happen on its own— different reading skills and their strategies will develop and be used at the appropriate time, and second language acquisition will result. Some care needs to be taken, however, in selecting texts and setting goals.

Choosing Reading Materials

Our guidelines for choosing readings to accompany a Natural Approach course follow from our earlier discussion of text appropriateness. Texts need not emphasize particular structures or vocabulary, but should simply aim at overall comprehensibility. As discussed earlier, students will be able to tolerate the inclusion of some grammar and vocabulary that is beyond their current level $(i+1)$. Moreover, the Input Hypothesis predicts that if the reading is comprehensible, the relevant structures $(i+1)$ and vocabulary will be present. Overcontrol of vocabulary and syntax is not only unnecessary, it is also detrimental, often resulting in a wooden, stilted style of writing.[20] It even runs the danger of denying the students the structure they might be ready for but that the writer may feel is too difficult.

Thus, overall comprehensibility meets the lexical and syntactic requirements for appropriateness in text difficulty. As mentioned earlier, semantic appropriateness requires a topic that is at least partly familiar and not overwhelmingly complex. And most important, the text needs to be of genuine interest.

To meet these requirements, we recommend that texts that accompany a Natural Approach class deal with topics similar to those discussed in class. Since our suggested syllabus in Chapter Four is an attempt to list topics of interest to students, readings can simply follow this list. The similarity of topic will facilitate comprehension for both reading and aural input in class.

Reading for the intermediate student, the student who has completed a Natural Approach course and who can read unedited texts to some extent, should follow the same principles of comprehensibility: at least partly familiar context, and interest. Krashen[21] recommends **narrow** and extensive reading, focussing on a single topic or author to take advantage of natural repetition of vocabulary and syntax as well as familiar context. Such an approach entails early, rather than late, specialization in the works of a single author in literature courses, and courses that focus on a single topic or series of related topics (as in "immersion" programs). Using narrow reading, acquirers can progress comfortably, gradually expanding the range of their reading.

Goals

We can influence the reader's search for meaning in a text by the sort of questions we ask. Some questions require only scanning, others require only skimming, while others may require intensive or extensive reading. The purpose of questions, in our view, is to encourage the use, and hence development, of the different skills.

Unfortunately, many questions typically asked of readers are aimed at none of the four skills, asking for detailed information that may be irrelevant to the central meaning of text. This type of question serves only to encourage the student to read every word and to pay attention to all details, a practice which may impede the development of efficient strategies and result in the overapplication of the intensive skill to all texts. It may even focus the student completely off the central meaning of the text. Been[22] gives a good example. Consider the sentence: *Mrs. Tse-Ling flies to the Occident twice a year to buy fashion clothes.* A correct answer to the question *"Where does Mrs. Tse-Ling go twice a year?"* can be provided without any knowledge of the meaning of the word "Occident"! Good questions focus the student on overall meaning and encourage the use of strategies that help the student find meaning.[23]

Some reading asssignments may actually require that the teacher not assign questions: it can be argued that questions of any sort take the pleasure out of pleasure reading! At least some, if not a great deal, of reading should be strictly voluntary and self-motivated [24], the teacher's role being only to provide the texts from which the student can make a selection.

It is sometimes argued that questions are necessary in order to provide practice on certain structures and vocabulary, the fear being that unless such practice is provided, these items will not be retained. But doing this can backfire: the extra drill may discourage further reading in the target language, thus insuring that the items of concern will indeed not be seen again. Good questions, on the other hand, focus readers on the essential message of the text, encourage the development of strategies and thus make subsequent reading easier, which in turn results in more second language acquisition.

Philip Hauptman [25] recommends the following rule of thumb to avoid over-detailed questions: read over the passage and then set it aside. Without looking at the passage again, list questions that appear to you to reflect the general sense of the passage. Hauptman's procedure, which seems very reasonable to us, prevents the teacher or materials developer from requiring more from the language acquirer than the educated native speaker can provide.

INTERVENTION

The reading program for the "natural reader" may not work for everyone; many students may need more help. Direct instruction in reading might be helpful for at least two kinds of students:

(1) Students who possess efficient reading strategies in their first language but who have failed to develop them in the second language. Such students often need "deprogramming", thanks to their experience in foreign language courses that demanded word-by-word intensive reading of difficult texts as the only reading experience.[26]

(2) Students who never developed efficient reading skills in their first language.[27]

A Philosophy of Intervention

Intervention, for us, means stimulating the development and use of efficient meaning-getting strategies in reading. Intervention programs may range from mild to heavy. Mild intervention programs will teach more general strategies, strategies that may unlock other, more specific strategies. Heavier programs will explicitly teach these specific strategies and will, in addition, provide more actual practice in their use. All intervention programs will contain lots of reading of appropriate texts, as described earlier.

Figure Two illustrates the mild to heavy progression. A mild intervention program could contain just the following two strategies:

1) Read for meaning.
2) Don't look up every word.

In our experience, merely stating these principles, with no further instructions or exercises, is often enough to "unlock" many readers who already read fluently in their first language.[28] (Such advice is, of course, useless if it is accompanied by the exclusive use of intensive reading assignments with detailed comprehension questions. It only works if reading assignments call for skimming, scanning and extensive reading, in addition to intensive work.)

FIGURE TWO
Reading Strategies

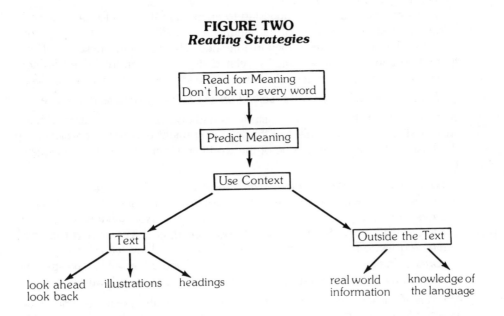

Slightly heavier intervention programs will teach a more specific strategy, the prediction of meaning, and may provide some practice. Goodman, Goodman and Flores make this suggestion:

> The teacher encourages readers to predict what is going to happen next at a particularly significant point in the story or article. Prior to the climax of a story, students suggest their own solutions and, after reading how the author solved the problem, discuss which of the various solutions they prefer and why. [29]

Pre-reading questions that help students focus on the crucial points of a passage may also serve to develop prediction strategies.

Another technique which has been reported to be successful in helping readers develop prediction strategies is the "cloze" technique. A "cloze" reading is one in which every *n*th word (usually *n* is between 5 and 10) is omitted and the reader must use the context in order to predict the missing word. As Hatch points out, the cloze procedure "(a) forces the reader to be active and constructive; (b) requires guesses based on both semantic and syntactic clues of the language; (c) requires retention of content in order for the reader to continue guessing." [30]

Still heavier intervention gives students more explicit help on using context. This can be of two kinds: (1) strategies that encourage readers to utilize information found in the text itself, and (2) strategies that use knowledge outside the text: the student's knowledge of the world and his knowledge of the language.

Text-related strategies are of several kinds. Some students may profit from being explicitly told to consider illustrations and headings in decoding the text. [31] In addition, students can be explicitly advised to look ahead in the text for cues to meaning of unfamiliar words.[32]

Exercises have also been suggested to encourage students to use real world information and knowledge of the language in addition to the text to predict meaning. The following examples are intended to help students make use of both text-related and outside knowledge-related strategies in an integrated fashion. Suppose, for example, that students found the following sentence in a passage:

John got out of his car and walked up the long pathway *to the house.*

Suppose further that none of the students had ever come into contact with the word *pathway.* Teacher-talk like the following might encourage prediction on the basis of the text, knowledge of the world and their acquired knowledge of English:

What sorts of words could be used after the expression "the long _____ ."
(Students will give an assortment of nouns like hair, arm, life, etc.) Yes, the plus a description demands the name of a thing after it. Now what sorts of things can we walk up? (Students suggest road, street, etc.) Yes. and in this case, where does John end up after walking? (The house). So what sorts of things connect the street, where he got out of his car and a house? (Some students may know the word sidewalk). Yes, a pathway *is like a sidewalk.*

At this point, it is not necessary that the students know the exact meaning of the word *pathway;* what is important is that they intuitively grasp the use of context to make an intelligent prediction of the meaning of the word. Indeed, it is often better that this sort of interchange does not end with a precise explanation of the word in question since this will lead the student to think that such detailed knowledge is necessary for comprehension of the passage in question. This is emphatically not the case; in fact, the following sort of teacher-talk is valuable to emphasize this:

We know that pathway *is similar to a* sidewalk. *Do we need to determine the exact meaning of* pathway? *No, why not? What are the important elements in this narrative? (John, leaves car, goes to house). Right. Thus, we can understand the essential elements of the narrative without understanding precisely how John arrived at the house.*

The use of immediate context was illustrated with the preceding example. However, another example of teacher talk will help illustrate the point more clearly:

The two thieves stood quietly in the underbrush.

In this case, the narrative deals with the execution of a robbery.

What sorts of words might describe ways of standing? How can we stand? (impatiently, restlessly, still, silently) What would be your guess at the meaning of the word in this context, that is, if you were a thief and were about to commit a robbery, would you make noise, or stand silently? So, the best guess is that quietly *means something like* silently. *What sorts of words can fit in the pattern in the* _____ ? *(street, building, river). Yes, words of location, of place, words which describe where someone is located. What is our guess here? In this case it is difficult to determine exactly where the robbers are (the meaning of* underbrush*) without more contextual information since thieves could logically be standing in many places. Let's read a bit further keeping in mind that we want to find out approximately where the thieves are standing.*

The narrative contiunues:

The leaves of the short bushes brushed against the jackets of the men as they tried to make as little noise as possible.

Teacher talk might be:

Does this sentence make it clearer where the men are standing? Are they inside a building? Not likely, since bushes are mostly found outdoors. What does this sentence tell us about the difficulty these two men are having with maintaining silence? (The leaves make noise.) Yes, then can we make an intelligent guess as to where the men are standing? (Among plants of some sort). Thus, underbrush *must refer to plants which grow outside. In fact, we will be able to tell more about the word* underbrush *as we read further looking for a clearer description of the place of the robbery.*

This kind of guidance may be superfluous to those students who are good readers in their first language and who transfer such inferencing techniques to the second language automatically. But, in our experience, many students can profit a great deal by this sort of explicit help in contextual prediction strategies. It should be also noted that such teacher-talk serves as comprehensible input for the acquisition process.

We wish to emphasize that prediction strategies will not always result in completely correct answers. But as Goodman points out "no readers read material they have not read before without errors...in the reading process accurate use of all clues available would not only be slow and inefficient, but would actually lead the reader away from his primary goal, which is comprehension." [33] Cates and Swaffer emphasize that the instructor "must strive therefore to reduce the learner's fear of error by removing the penalty for...local errors and by stating plainly that some wrong inferences are unavoidable but that without inferences, reading is impossible." [34]

Evidence for Intervention

There is only suggestive evidence that the kind of intervention we are proposing does, in fact, result in better reading in a second language. Swaffer and

Woodruff reported that extensive reading along with deliberate teaching of strategies resulted in improvement in college-level German. Some of the exercise types used included "selection of three to five sentences that pinpoint the main events of the text...elimination in selected sentences of words that are not essential for understanding the main idea...cloze readings, in which every fifth to tenth word is left out and students choose a plausible word from a list to fill the blank..." [35] On the other hand, Newmark [36] used extensive reading alone and apparently had excellent results with a similar population. All we can conclude from this research is that proper reading experience probably does encourage the development of good strategies, and it is also possible that intervention has an effect for many students. Clearly, studies need to be done that compare different approaches directly.

First language reading does appear to be facilitated by instruction and practice of the sort described here. This includes cloze practice of certain kinds. Sampson, Valmont and Van Allen [37], in a recent study using third graders, emphasize the value of discussion of possible answers with the teacher, for example. Also, Hansen [38], in a study using second graders, found that "a pre-reading strategy in which children utilized previous experiences to predict events" was helpful.

Even if intervention is shown to be successful in helping second language performers develop good strategies, the cornerstone of any reading program remains the reading itelf, texts at an appropriate level of difficulty of genuine interest to readers. The job of the class is not only to provide such texts for actual reading practice, but also to help the student find reading outside the class, so progress in the second language will continue after the course ends. The availability of outside reading has been shown to be a strong predictor of reading ability in both first and second language. [39] Our goal should be to show the students where this reading is, and to put them in a position to make use of it.

TEACHING FOR MONITOR USE

In Chapters Two and Three, we stressed the notion that there are two ways of gaining knowledge used to communicate in a second language; we have called these acquisition and learning. The theory of second language acquisition which we have proposed relates these two sources of language skill in a particular way: acquired knowledge is used to generate utterances while learned knowledge serves primarily a monitoring function. For this reason, classroom activities to facilitate acquisition play a dominant role in the Natural Approach classroom. Indeed, Chapters Four and Five were devoted to describing the sorts of activities which encourage acquisition rather than learning. This does not mean, however, that learning activities do not have a place in the Natural Approach. They do, but they do not assume the dominant role which they have in other approaches such as cognitive or audiolingual.

Let us consider briefly the function of learning exercises for each of the three types of students we described in Chapter Two: the under-users, the over-users and the optimal users. Under-users either cannot (or make no effort to) use knowledge which is learned. (Sometimes these are students who say they have no "knack" for grammar.) These students generally have to rely almost completely on acquisition for their language skills. For over-users, we will want to de-emphasize learning exercises since their over-reliance on them typically interferes with both their attempts to communicate and with the acquisition process itself. Our goal is to try to make both under-users and over-users into optimal users, those who use what they have learned to facilitate communication and to supplement their acquired competence.[40]

On the other hand, the idea of optimal Monitor use is not absolute. The level of ability to monitor successfully will vary from student to student and will depend on several factors. Our experience has been that students with background in grammar study in their native language are often able to monitor more successfully than those with little such experience. In these cases, the instructor and students will have to make decisions about the relative amount of time that will be dedicated to learning exercises to develop the ability to monitor.

The danger, of course, is to overestimate the value of learning exercises. Keep in mind that even if the students know particular rules and forms, these can only be successfully monitored given focus on correctness. Even students who are fully capable of learning the most complex grammatical principles will not be able to utilize their knowledge very often in communicative situations. Our recommendation is that students bring in the conscious grammar only in situations where it will not interfere with communication, as in writing or prepared speech. Overappeal to complex rules in conversation, for example, will result in a hesitant, overcareful style that is difficult to listen to, and may also encourage "planning while the other person is talking," which endangers the success of the entire interaction.

A recommendation that monitoring in normal conversation not be emphasized has consequences for the classroom interactions. Monitoring during normal conversation is difficult even for the most proficient of Monitor users. There is simply not usually enough time to comprehend what is heard, to think of an appropriate response, to generate the response and to self-correct under the constraints of rapid conversational interchange. This is especially true if the speaker must monitor phonology, a great deal of bound morphology, and syntax that is radically different from the speaker's native language. Therefore, speech errors must be accepted as a natural part of the acquisition process.

Monitoring will also assume different levels of importance in different stages of acquisition. It is clear that children are not capable of much conscious monitoring with learned knowledge. Adults, at least theoretically, can utilize learned knowledge a great deal more than can children. Beginners of any age have very little use for monitoring; indeed, too much use of grammar in early acquisition stages is often detrimental since the speaker may spend so much time processing rules and forms that he misses the messge being conveyed, thereby hindering the acquisition process. On the other hand, intermediates and advanced students of a second language, those who can communicate fairly well and who normally understand most of what is said to them, might well profit by concentrating on learning aspects of morphology and syntax that are normally very late acquired, thereby giving their speech a more polished sound, and their written output a more correct form.

There are two phases in the presentation of material which is to be learned: (1) explanation; (2) practice.

Grammar Explanation

The explanation can come from the instructor and/or from a text.[41] We prefer to avoid oral grammar explanations in the classroom simply because they take time away from acquisition activities. Thus, in cases in which the student can profitably use a grammar text outside the classroom, such use is recommended. If there are questions about the material in the text, the instructor should, by all means, try to answer them to clear up any confusion. (Monitoring is impossible if the students do not understand the rule.) If grammar explanations are done in the classroom, we recommend that they be short, simple and in the target language. This is, of course, a necessity in classes with different first languages or in classes in which the instructor does not speak the language of the students. We can imagine foreign language classes in which a very short explanation in the native language could be acceptable. In general, however, we prefer explanations in the target language. First, the language of the explanation can serve as input for acquisition if it is comprehensible. Second, if the explanation is so complex that it cannot be understood from an explanation in the target language, there is a good possibility that the rule in question is too complex to be learned at this stage, and the explanation should be postponed until more acquisition (and perhaps learning) has taken place.

Learning Exercises

We will consider in this section the use of exercises aimed at the teaching of grammar, i.e., syntax and morphology.[42] There are three principle types of learning exercises: (1) Written grammar drills of the sort used in grammar courses; (2) audiolingual drills, and (3) communicative grammar drills.

Written grammar exercises are found in any standard textbook. They usually focus on a particular grammar rule and force the students to apply the rule over and over in a given exercise. Very common are morphology exercises in which the student need only supply the correct form.

Choose the correct past tense form:

    a. I_____to the store. (run)
    b. The boy_____a new shirt. (choose)

Such exercises are particularly common in language courses in which the language being studied is morphologically complex. For example, students of

French and Spanish are usually required to do these sorts of exercises to drill the person-number and tense forms of the verb systems.

Choose the correct verb form:

    a. Yo _____ español todos los días. (estudiar)
    b. Mi amigo _____ a las doce. (comer)

Or, they practice various rules of agreement, gender-number agreement in the noun phrase, for example:

Choose the correct form:

    a. C'est _____ _____ jeune fille.
          (un, une) (beau, belle)
    b. Voilà _____ livre _____ .
       (le, la)   (gris, grise)

Exercises to teach syntax usually consist of transformations and sentence combining:

Combine the following sentence to make a single sentence with a relative clause.

    a. This is my sister. She lives in Kansas.
       (This is my sister who lives in Kansas.)
    b. He found the note. I left him the note.
       (He found the note that I left him.)

In many languages, such transformations often involve complex morphological choices. For example, in the Romance languages, dependent clauses often result in a choice between Indicative and Subjunctive moods.

Combine the following sentences; pay attention to correct choice of mood.

    a. Juan no estudia mucho. Es necesario.
       (Es necesario que Juan estudie mucho.)
    b. Usted vendrá mañana. Lo quiero.
       (Quiero que usted venga mañana.)

Audiolingual drills are normally presented orally and are often used to practice the manipulation of form (usually morphological changes such as agreement rules) or syntax (for example, clause combining or other simple transformations). The vocabulary and sentence patterns are held constant so that the students can focus on the changes required. They are usually done with the following procedure: the instructor gives the pattern sentence which is repeated by the students, then the cue or new pattern is given by the instructor and the sentence is transformed by the students. The instructor repeats the correct answer which is repeated again by the students.

The following audiolingual drill from a textbook for beginning students of Spanish is typical.[43]

    MODEL   ¿No fuiste tú a la venta?

STUDENT   ¿No fue él a la venta?

1. ¿No fuiste tú a la venta?	2. Jose Marti fue poeta.	3. Mónica le dio el traje viejo.
Rosa	Juana	Uds.
Rosa y Carlos	Yo	Nosotras
ellas	Tú	Tú
yo	Tú y yo	El
Ud.	Nosotros	El y ella

In this drill the student's attention is directed to the rule of subject-verb agreement in Spanish. To be practiced is the irregular past tense conjugation of *to go, to be,* and *to give*. The substitutions to be performed orally consist of subject pronouns or names of people, i.e., a minimum amount of semantic material in order for the student to concentrate strictly on the rule of subject-verb agreement. Since this is a pattern drill, the same sentence pattern is maintained throughout a single substitution drill so that the student is not distracted by a multitude of meanings.

Communicative drills differ from grammar exercises and audiolingual drills only in that they attempt to give the material the student is working with a realistic context and perhaps a purpose. The following is a typical example of a communicative audiolingual drill.

> Your friend Marie is visiting. Ask her if she wants to go to the following places.
> Example: Beach. Do you want to go to the beach?
> (1) lake   (2) movies   (3) park   (4) mountains
> (5) grocery store   (6) shopping center.

In the following example the students practice the past tense forms.

> Tell your Mom that you and your friends did the following things yesterday:
> (1) go shopping   (2) eat at a restaurant   (3) finish the homework
> (4) study in the library   (5) play baseball.

All three types of exercises, grammar exercises, audiolingual drills, and communicative drills, can be valuable as tools to encourage learning. However, it should be kept in mind that while their function is important, very little acquisition will take place during their use. In addition, grammar exercises and audiolingual drills have inherent problems associated with their use. For example, the following exercise is typical in textbooks for beginners.[44]

> Make the subjects and verbs plural.
> 1. No quiero ir.
> 2. ¿Quiere usted ir al cine?
> 3. El toma mucha aspirina.
> 4. ¿Tiene usted que estudiar?
> 5. Ella no lo sabe.

6. Pongo la fruta en la mesa.
7. Mi amigo sale de su casa a las ocho.
8. El tiene más que yo.
9. El médico examina al paciente.
10. El paciente paga al médico.

In this exercise the student is to change singular subject noun phrases into plural noun phrases with concomitant verb agreement. It seems to us that extensive practice with such rules is of dubious value to the average beginning student. It is true that practice of this sort of exercise might result in the learning, but not acquisition, of this rule. The problem is that there is little or no chance for aquisition of this or any other rule in this exercise due to the extreme mixture of disparate potential messages. The topic jumps randomly from a question about going someplace, to taking aspirin and from studying, to putting fruit on the table. It is extremely doubtful that even the most dedicated student could maintain a focus on the ever-changing meaning of these sentences. This, of course, is in addition to the inherent tedium in such exercises.

Audiolingual drills suffer from similar problems. First, the fact that such drills are oral creates tension in the class. Second, the simplification done to maintain the focus on a single grammatical element, creates a great deal of boredom which is hard to overcome even by the most dedicated of instructors and students. Consider the following substitution drill aimed at practicing gender and number agreement in Spanish.

Tengo un libro bueno.	Tengo un libro bueno.
_____ mesa _____ .	Tengo una mesa buena.
_____ dos _____ .	Tengo dos mesas buenas.
_____ cuaderno ____ .	Tengo un cuaderno bueno.
_____buenos.	Tengo unos cuadernos buenos.

Since attention is focused on gender and number agreement, these rules might be learned, but certainly not acquired. If at the same time, however, the students keep in mind the meaning of what they are repeating, perhaps other aspects of form and structure (in this case perhaps word order, and the verb form *tengo* 'I have') might be advancing in the acquisition process. Thus, such exercises may not be completely useless for acquisition even though they are not particularly efficient. Unfortunately, audiolingual drills are often excruciatingly boring for both the instructor and the students and if used extensively they may contribute more to negative feelings about language study than to the learning of the rule in question.

Communication drills are closest to acquisition activities in that there are potential messages to be communicated. Despite their label, however, communicative drills remain grammar exercises, and this focus on form prevents full focus on the message. The Input Hypothesis thus predicts that little acquisition will result from communicative drills. We recommend, in general, that one should not depend on learning activities to provide input for acquisition. What acquisition does take place in learning-oriented classes may be largely the result of the language of explanation, the teacher-talk, rather than the exercises.[45]

The Balance Between Acquisition Activities and Learning Exercises

We have tried to indicate in the discussion in this section that there are several factors which will determine the specific balance of acquisition and learning activities to be used in the Natural Approach. We will review these quickly and then make specific recommendations.

The most important consideration is the goal of the course. If, as discussed earlier, students already communicate well in the target language and wish to supplement their acquired competence, some time can be spent on learning exercises. Learning will be useful to these students in writing and in prepared speech, and give their output a "polished" look. Some students are interested in the structure of language for its own sake. For these students, grammar can be taught as subject matter. Such study does not directly help second language proficiency. If a course in grammar is taught in the second language, however, the instructor's speech will provide comprehensible input and help acquisition.[46]

It is the assumption of this book that acquisition activities are fundamental in taking students who have no knowledge of the target language to the point at which they can understand native speakers and communicate their thoughts and desires. For these students, both children and adults, acquisition activities are both necessary and sufficient. Learning activities will be used judiciously and in some cases not at all.

For students of all ages, we recommend that learning activities not begin until the students have progressed through the prespeaking and one-word stages, i.e., until they are starting to produce at least short sentences. For children, acquisition activities will continue to dominate the class and learning activities will be used primarily in learning to write. For adolescents and most adults, we recommend that at least 80% of the course be devoted to acquisition activities and only 20% or less be given to learning exercises.

What Can be Monitored?

We have suggested that only a relatively small part of the grammar of a language can be learned for monitoring.[47] While there is considerable individual variation, even the "best" adult Monitor users confine most of their monitoring to the simpler grammatical rules—inflections and very simple order changes. Complex permutations require too much mental energy and processing time. Also, performers do not need to Monitor rules that are already acquired. Thus, the "grammar" portion of the course need only concern itself with simpler, late acquired rules if the goal is improvement of the Monitor.

Thanks to the Natural Order phenomenon, we do not have to determine empirically the set of rules to be taught to each student—what is "late acquired" for one student will usually be late acquired for another. In English, for example, we can safely assume that the third-person singular, regular past, and possessive 's will be late acquired for each new group of students. Since these are also relatively straightforward rules, they are good rules to teach deliberately.

To repeat, grammar teaching of these kinds of rules is justified if it is used only in situations in which the conditions for Monitor use are met — when there is time, a focus on form, and when the rules have been studied. We should not expect our students to apply learned rules consistently in spontaneous oral performance. We must not forget that accuracy in oral output comes mainly from acquisition, after a great deal of comprehensible input.

WRITING

Writing Goals

We have tried to emphasize that the main focus of the Natural Approach is providing comprehensible input for language acquisition. The students' own output is theoretically secondary with regard to the acquisition process. Oral output, speech, is indirectly useful in that it helps to encourage aural input, i.e., conversation. It is therefore useful for acquisition for the student to speak the target language after some competence has been built up via input. We cannot make the same sort of argument for writing. Writing does not necessarily encourage comprehensible input, unless acquirers are exchanging letters or notes.

Writing may, of course, be an additional goal of a course in which the Natural Approach is being used to impart oral communication skills. For example, students of English who intend to do a college degree in an English-speaking country need highly developed writing skills. On the other hand, there are language courses in which writing skills are irrelevant. A Latin American student from Brazil, for example, who wishes to travel a bit in France, may want to learn enough oral French to communicate basic travel needs, but may be entirely uninterested in learning to write French. The inclusion of a writing component is thus dependent more on the goals and needs of the students rather than on its methodological usefulness for the development of oral communication skills.

There are four possible reasons for including writing in a Natural Approach class: (1) to record and review vocabulary in the prespeaking stage, (2) as an integral part of an oral activity which provides comprehsible input, (3) as practice in monitoring, and (4) as a practical goal. We will examine each separately.

Writing in the Prespeaking Stage

As we noted in Chapter Four, if students are literate adults, it is possible that copying important vocabulary words that the instructor writes on the chalkboard during comprehension activities will help them remember the meanings of the words, as well as the sound-letter correspondences.[48] Many adults are so accustomed to working with written language that a completely oral experience is often very difficult to adjust to; thus, writing may have important affective implications.

The writing of key words can have some adverse effects, such as overdependence on the written word or interference in pronunciation because of some native language orthographic correspondences. These problems are, however, counteracted by Natural Approach techniques. In the first place, only key items are written on the chalkboard, forcing students to rely mainly on what they hear for interpretation of meaning. In the second place, students are normally not asked to speak the target language until they have been exposed to it for several hours. Such techniques reduce native language influence.

Writing and Oral Production

Writing can also play a role in many of the activities in which the goal is oral production. In the open-ended sentence model, the open dialog model, and the interview model (see Chapter Four), students may be instructed to write their answers before giving them orally. Writing may also be a part of games. For example, in one game students write down all of the words they can find on a sheet of scrambled letters. In a content activity, students might be asked to write a sentence describing what they see in each of a set of slides on some cultural aspect. Or they might be asked to write a reaction to some work of art or music. In affective-humanistic activities, writing can often be very helpful. In the following example, each student must interview another student and fill out the required information.

PASSPORT APPLICATION

Name _____

Address _____

Place of birth _____

Date of birth _____

Countries wish to travel to _____

Reason for travel _____

In the following activity for a Spanish class, students are asked to fill in a chart with personal descriptions of their fellow students (eye color, hair color, clothing, favorite course, year in school):

	Compañero 1	Compañero 2	Compañero 3
Nombre			
Color de los ojos			
Color del pelo			
Ropa que lleva			
Curso favorito			
Nivel escolar			

Problem-solving activities very frequently involve writing: [49]

Using the information in the chart, write a biography of each person in paragraph form.

NAME	DATE OF BIRTH	EDUCATION	YEAR OF MARRIAGE	OCCUPATION	DATE OF DEATH
Henry Peterson	12/5/01	New York University	1929, 1940	advertising director	7/7/77
Diane Denton	4/30/45	Wellington College	—	TV and movie actress	10/25/75
Oscar Gomez	1/14/25	University of California	1958	sportswriter	2/3/78
Elena Economopoulou	8/27/19	Miss Flower's School	1937; 1957	company director	3/17/76

1. *Henry Peterson was born on December 5, 1901. He studied at New York University. His first marriage was in 1929, and his second marriage was in 1940. He was an advertising director. He died on July 7, 1977.*

2. _____

   _____

   _____

   _____

First the students write the indicated paragraphs; follow-up is oral. Normally such an activity would then be extended to apply to students in the class, with one student interviewing another and then writing a similar paragraph on the information obtained.

In all of these cases, writing is not an end in itself but is preliminary to the execution of an activity whose central purpose is to provide an opportunity to interact and gain comprehensible input.

Writing to Practice Monitoring

We have stressed the fact that the Monitor can be used only in restricted circumstances: the student must know the rule, be focused on correctness and have time to apply the rule. In normal conversation, as we have said, these conditions are rarely met and monitoring is neither particularly easy nor practical. In written work, however, it is possible to supply all three prerequisites.

There are two different sorts of circumstances in which monitoring can be practiced in writing. First, it is appropriate to monitor carefully when writing grammar exercises aimed at learning rules. The focus in these exercises is normally a single grammatical point which the student is presumably aware of. Second, the instructor can encourage the students to monitor at appropriate times in their creative written work. For example, in any work in which the student is to generate original sentences, such as writing a paragraph or answering questions about a reading, initial production is mostly dependent on the acquired system just as is speech. But with written production, there is time to edit what the acquired system has produced. We recommend that instructors encourage free rein of the acquired system during actual composing, but that, afterwards, students be encouraged to edit using conscious rules. They will not be able to correct every error this way but will be able to significantly increase their written accuracy.[50]

For example, cartoons can serve as a stimulus for the construction of original narratives. This example[51] is especially good because the pictures can be

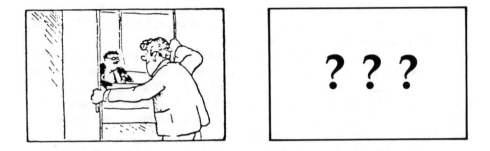

arranged in several different orders resulting in different narratives. This sort of writing exercise results in connected narration with only very general instructions. After the narrative has been written, the instructor can ask the students to edit (monitor) what they have produced. A reminder of what rules they are to monitor can be helpful: look for subject-verb agreement, tense errors, article and preposition usage, and so forth.

Functional Writing Goals

Finally, writing can, in certain circumstances, be an appropriate goal in its own right in a second language course. In this case, writing activities will correspond directly to writing needs. If students need to learn to write business letters in English, for example, these skills will have to be practiced directly. Others may need to learn to write technical reports or even extensive essays on various topics. Certainly students who will study in a second language need highly developed writing skills. This can be done via a great deal of reading of appropriate documents to acquire the specific "styles" and writing exercises that encourage the conscious learning of late acquired but necessary aspects of each writing style.

TELEVISION AND RADIO AS INPUT SOURCES

Television is available to students of many languages, but infrequently taken advantage of. Broadcasts completely in the target language are difficult for beginners, but not impossible. We suggest beginning with short advertisement spots. The instructor first videotapes a series of these spots. In the classroom, the instructor plays a single spot which usually lasts less than a minute. Since the visual image is present, the students will at least understand the context of the communication. The instructor then asks the students to listen to the spot again and concentrate on key words they do understand. The instructor then asks a single question about one item of information in the commercial, asking students to concentrate on figuring out the answer to just that one question. Normally, at least one student will be successful. This exercise is repeated with several other key questions. With each question, important vocabulary items are written on the board to facilitate further comprehension. A replaying of the commercial at this point should result in some comprehension for most of the students. The key to success in all listening activities is to concentrate on understanding the main points without trying to identify every word.

Programs of various sorts can be worked with in similar fashion. The crucial point, however, is to find short meaningful intervals. Skits on variety shows or parts of news broadcasts lend themselves well to this. What does not work for beginners is to play a tape of 30 minutes or so without pause and then expect the students to discuss the contents. The input will be so far above their levels that almost none of it will be comprehensible.

Radio resources can be used similarly. The main difference is that there is no video image to help with comprehension. On the other hand, there is the advantage that in radio there are many varied announcements and other short items which lend themselves well to a classroom activity or even as a homework assignment. Radio advertisement spots can be taught in the same way as television commercials. After some classroom practice, it is easy to assign these commercials as homework. To do this activity, the instructor prepares a list of key vocabulary items and phrases in the broadcast. In a short commercial there should be not more than 15-20 new key words. To this list is added a set of questions which, when answered, will demonstrate that the student has comprehended the commercial. Some students will understand the recorded material after two or three repetitions, others may need up to thirty repetitions. Since each student is working on the assignment individually, the number of repetitions need not affect the outcome. Students using the Natural Approach report a good deal of improvement in listening comprehension after several of these sorts of activities. Similar techniques can be done with radio news broadcasts and other programs. The goal is for the students to learn how to listen well and realize that they can understand, even with limited information and knowledge. This understanding hopefully will encourage further listening and more input.

HOMEWORK

Extensive homework assignments are possible only in certain restricted academic situations. With children and often with working adults, we must be satisfied with what can be accomplished within the class period. On the other hand, if the language is taught in the area in which it is spoken, or if a sizeable number of speakers of the language live nearby, often assignments can be made to take advantage of these resources. We will have more to say about this possibility in the section "Modification for Second Language Instruction" in the next chapter.

Homework can be classified into three types: (1) activities that provide more comprehensible input, to supplement class offerings; (2) activities that provide the student with routines and phrases that help conversational management, and (3) activities that build a Monitor, i.e., to learn rules.

Under the first category, we recommend pleasure reading in the target language, with an emphasis on extensive, not intensive, reading. Of course, we also recommend conversations with speakers of the language, if they are available. Radio and TV can provide excellent supplementary sources of input. Beginning students may have trouble with all of these, but with some class preparation, of the sort described in the previous sections, the exercises can be successful. In addition, some of the acquisition activities we described in Chapter Five can serve as homework assignments.

Home may also be the appropriate place for the practice and optional memorization of short dialogs that contain routines and phrases that may be helpful in conversation. Such dialogs should be extremely short and maximally useful. The classroom will then provide situations in which to practice these memorized routines and patterns.

Finally, learning activities for Monitor practice are probably most efficiently done outside of class.

VOCABULARY

Vocabulary is basic to communication. If acquirers do not recognize the meanings of the key words used by those who address them, they will be unable to participate in the conversation. And if they wish to express some idea or ask for information, they must be able to produce lexical items to convey their meaning. Indeed, if our students know the morphology and syntax of an utterance addressed to them, but do not know the meanings of the key lexical items, they will be unable to participate in the communication. For this reason, we are not impressed with approaches that deliberately restrict vocabulary acquisition and learning until the morphology and syntax are mastered.

Vocabulary is also very important for the acquisition process. The popular belief is that one uses form and grammar to understand meaning. The truth is probably closer to the opposite: we acquire morphology and syntax because we understand the meaning of utterances. Acquisition depends crucially on the input being comprehensible. And comprehensibility is dependent directly on the ability to recognize the meaning of key elements in the utterance. Thus, acquisition will not take place without comprehension of vocabulary.

The Role of Vocabulary in Natural Approach Stages

The prespeaking stage is characterized by nearly complete attention to vocabulary recognition. Indeed, the purpose of the prespeaking stage is for the students to develop listening strategies based primarily on lexical item recognition. Students listen to input which is so highly contextualized that they can focus on key lexical items and interpret the general meaning of the utterances produced by the instructor. Since the activities concentrate solely on listening skills, the ability to recognize the meaning of words in context can be expanded quite rapidly. Our experience has shown that children participating in the sorts of Natural Approach activities described in Chapter Four can acquire, for recognition (interpretive) purposes, about 15 to 25 new lexical items per hour, while adults can often acquire up to 50 words per hour of comprehensible input. In methods which require instant production of new lexical items, these figures are greatly reduced.[52]

Rapid rate of acquisition of a recognition vocabulary is especially useful for children who are acquiring the language which is, or will be, the medium of instruction. These students need to be in a position to understand input in classrooms and on the playground as soon as possible. A large recognition vocabulary will contribute a great deal to their classroom success, their social life, and to their continuing acquisition of the target language.

Vocabulary continues to play a dominant role in the early speech stage. Indeed, as students begin to produce one- and two-word utterances, the instructor expands the input with new vocabulary. As the students become increasingly able to recognize familiar words without depending on context, these words themselves then become part of the context, thus allowing the acquirers to interpret new lexical items.

Finally, as speech emerges, vocabulary remains important as the students begin to expand their range of interaction in the target language to new topics and new situations.

Teaching Vocabulary

The Natural Approach is based on the premise that vocabulary is acquired via comprehensible input; new words are acquired when they are heard in an utterance or in a sentence that is comprehensible. Thus, our classroom acquisition activities aim at continual comprehension of new lexical items in a communicative context.

As we have said many times in this book, in all of these activities the focus remains on understanding messages. Just as a particular affective acquisition activity, for example, may entail the use of certain grammatical structures, the activity is not designed to "teach" that structure. The same is true of vocabulary; activities are not necessarily "vocabulary builders". Students' attention is not on vocabulary learning per se but on communication, on the goal of an activity. In this way, we encourage true vocabulary acquisition.

It may be argued that a Natural Approach to vocabulary acquisition is impractical, in that classroom time is limited and that only a small range of topics can be discussed. Thus, some intervention in the form of more direct teaching, such as rote learning or vocabulary exercises, is necessary. There is no evidence, however, that such intervention helps much. It appears to be the case that "memorized" or "drilled" vocabulary does not stick; words learned by rote or drill do not enter permanent memory storage.[53] True vocabulary acquisition with long-term retention occurs only with meaningful exposure in situations in which real communication takes place.

Pre-teaching Vocabulary

In at least one circumstance, deliberate vocabulary teaching, that is, exercises or activities which are deliberately focused on the meanings of new words, can be useful in helping acquisition. This involves presentation and explanation of certain key words preceding a discussion or acquisition activity. For example, as we noted earlier, instructors may prepare short lists of key vocabulary words in preparing students to understand radio commercials. Immersion classes, in which subject matter is taught through the medium of a second language, often use this technique, with the teacher explaining important vocabulary before the lesson begins.

Such pre-teaching may or may not lead to the acquisition of the specific words presented. It will, however, help to make the activity itself more comprehensible and thus help acquisition of other items and/or structures.

The goal of the Natural Approach is to provide enough vocabulary to allow language use outside the classroom, and to place the student in a position to continue second language acquisition. Meeting this goal entails developing a substantial recognition vocabulary and a sufficiently large production vocabulary so that the student can participate in a variety of interpersonal communicative situations. It does not entail trying to prepare students in advance with every word they might meet in their future language use. Such preparation is neither practical nor necessary. If our students are able to communicate with native speakers, and read for interest and pleasure, even if they do not understand every word, vocabulary will continue to grow.[54][55]

Notes

1. The hypothesis that reading may contribute to performance in other modalities is consistent with Oller's hypothesis (Oller 1981) that a large general factor underlies different tasks in second language testing. While a single factor does not account for all the variance in language performance, Oller concludes that the general factor is very strong. Bachman and Palmer's work, cited in Oller (1981) shows that there is clear evidence for separate reading and writing factors; nevertheless, performance across modalities is strongly correlated and the existence of a robust general factor is well supported.
2. Grittner 1977.
3. Grittner 1977, pp. 250-1.
4. See e.g. Cohen et. al. 1979.
5. Schlesinger 1968.
6. Ulijn and Kempen 1976.
7. See also MacNamara 1967, cited in Hatch 1974.
8. Hatch 1979, p. 137.
9. For a review of research in aural comprehension in first language, see Clark and Clark 1977, pp. 72-79.
10. Omaggio (1979) confirmed that context plays a helpful role. In her study, college level students of French as a foreign language read passages that were accompanied by one of several pictures. The picture that was the most useful in helping students understand the story was one that depicted a scene from the beginning of the story. Omaggio suggests that the picture served as an "advance organizer" and helped the reader organize his existing store of knowledge before reading.
11. The "rule of forgetting", Krashen 1982a.
12. Unfortunately, using different reading skills for different purposes has not always been recognized. For example, Meras 1954, p. 158, stated that "the ultimate objective is obviously complete and accurate understanding of the passage that is read. An approximate or superficial understanding is not enough either in a beginning or advanced class. Every reading lesson must provide complete comprehension."
13. Goodman 1967.
14. A similar process takes place in aural comprehension. There are, however, some differences: in aural comprehension, for example, perceivers cannot regress to go over old material easily, i.e., "reread" (Goodman 1971, p. 137). Aural input is typically embedded in a more "context-rich" situation, which helps comprehension (Cummins 1981; Goodman 1971). Also, feedback from the conversational partner is available in aural comprehension, which is not available in reading.
15. Goodman 1971, p. 139.
16. Figure One assumes, perhaps incorrectly, that language acquisition can result from the use of any of the four skills. This may not be so; scanning, for example, may be so independent of the grammatical structure used in a text that the scanner may never read comprehensible messages encoded with i+1. This is, however, an empirical question.
17. Cziko reported that the performance of advanced (early French immersion) students on cloze tests was significantly better for normal passages than for passages violating French discourse constraints. (Texts violating discourse constraints appear grammatical but do not deal with a topic coherently.) Intermediate (late immersion) students did not perform significantly better on the normal passage, indicating less ability to take advantage of the overall context in reading for meaning. Hauptmann's research (Hauptman 1981) is also consistent with these results. Less advanced adult students of French made more syntactic errors on a cloze test, while more advanced students made more errors relating to semantics. Hauptman speculates that this result is due to the more advanced students being more willing "to take a chance". If so, he points out (p. 50) that this is a "positive L2 reading strategy" since it entails more hypothesis-making and hypothesis-testing, and less reliance on the text itself.

18. Cited in Hatch 1974.
19. Cohen et. al. 1979, p. 559.
20. See discussion in Stevick 1980, Chapter 16, and Krashen 1982a, Chapter Three.
21. Krashen 1982b.
22. Been 1975.
23. See also Cates and Swaffer 1979, pp. 8-10.
24. For discussion and evidence from first language acquisition, see Krashen (forthcoming)
25. Philip Hauptman, personal communication.
26. Note that some good first language readers who read poorly in the second language may simply need more second language acquisition. Clark (1980) reports that low level second language performers who are good first language readers do not use the efficient reading strategies that they use in first language reading. Many such performers will develop good second language reading skills with more second language acquisition.
27. It is interesting to note that poor first language reading may be caused by factors similar to those posited to cause poor reading in the second language: over-emphasis on word-by-word processing, decoding individual letters, overattention to detail and discouraging guessing (see e.g. Smith 1975; Spitzer 1975).
28. Students often feel they should look up each unknown word for two reasons: they may think it is necessary in order to understand the text and they think it will help them learn new vocabulary. The first reason is false with respect to a surprising number of words, as discussed earlier. The second reason is not true either—in fact, overuse of the dictionary may actually impede acquisition of vocabulary, since it slows down reading so much. (We even know of people who will not pleasure read in a second language because they feel this need to look up every word and they dread the work involved!) Vocabulary acquisition does not depend exclusively on the bilingual dictionary. The meanings of many words are acquired by context, by their appearance in comprehensible messages. For many types of reading, for scanning, skimming and extensive reading, very little use of the dictionary is necessary; the dictionary should be reserved for those cases in which a word's meaning appears to be absolutely necessary for comprehension of the text and context is insufficient. Edward Finegan (personal communication) reports success with a system which can be called the "annoyance system": look up words whose meanings are still unacquired despite considerable exposure, i.e., words whose appearance "annoys" you!
29. Goodman, Goodman and Flores 1979, p. 38.
30. Hatch 1979, p. 140.
31. See e.g. Hauptman 1982 and Hosenfeld, Arnold, Kirchofer, Laciura and Wilson 1981.
32. The importance of "looking ahead" has been confirmed by Homburg and Spaan 1982 in a study of university-age ESL students. Those who performed best in reading for overall meaning in a cloze-type task also employed more of this forward-looking strategy, using context following an unknown word to infer its meaning.
33. Goodman 1971, p. 139.
34. Cates and Swaffer 1979, p. 6.
35. Swaffer and Woodruff 1978, pp. 28-29.
36. Newmark 1971.
37. Sampson, Valmont and Van Allen 1982.
38. Hansen 1981.
39. For first language, see Thorndike 1973. For second language, see Williams 1981.
40. It is important to note that learning does not "become" acquisition, nor does it help acquisition (Krashen, 1982a). Acquired competence comes only from comprehensible input. Conscious rules do not become subconscious via output, or production practice. Conscious learning is only useful to the performer as a temporary supplement to acquisition, and is available only when the conditions for Monitor use, as presented in Chapter Two, are met.
41. Grammar explanation is a common practice in most methodologies. Explanation may be oral by the instructor or written in the text or both. The instructor may use an inductive

approach in which the students are led stepwise through examples to discover a rule, or deductive, in which the instructor simply explains the rule and them gives the students examples on which to practice applications.

42. Learning exercises may also teach phonology, vocabulary, semantics, pragmatics and other rules of communicative competence. We have concentrated on morphology and syntax since these are the most common components taught in language classes.

43. From Keller 1979.

44. From Crow 1979, p. 100.

45. Note that all grammar exercises illustrated here are of one sort: "output plus error correction". The student *produces* something and is then told whether it was correct. This is quite the opposite of what is actually necessary for acquisition, *input* with attention directed to meaning, and not form.

46. See discussion in Krashen 1981, p. 118, Krashen 1982a, pp. 119-121. Interestingly, intensive and detailed grammar study may lower the filter for students who find it interesting, but raise the filter for others.

47. Some critics maintain that approaches such as ours, which seem to stress communication over accuracy, will result in "bad habits": a permanently fossilized pidgin-like language. The writers usually, but not always (see e.g. Higgs and Clifford 1981) suggest that formal grammar exercises is the antidote for the syndrome of fluent but "sloppy" language.

It is undeniably true that Natural Approach students make speech errors. They show "developmental" errors, errors that reveal the operation of the language acquisition device (see discussion in Chapter Two). Many of these errors in the adult, and all, in the case of children, usually disappear with more comprehensible input. It is our experience that students studying with other methods would show more of these errors if allowed to express themselves (for some interesting examples, see Felix 1981).

Research also indicates that students taught according to "comprehensible input" methods do as well on formal tests of grammar (or better) than students taught using grammar-based methods, and do significantly better in measures of communication fluency (see Voge 1981, Bushman and Madsen, 1976 and other studies cited in Chapter Two). The latter result suggests that students who are taught using communicative-comprehensible input methods will be more prone to interact and will thus have a better chance of improving on their own.

Fossilization, we maintain, does not result from bad habits, nor can it be cured by drill or conscious learning. According to the theory outlined in Chapter Two, it results from a lack of appropriate input and/or a too strong Affective Filter. Cases of the former type exist even among long-term residents of a country who use the second language daily. Quite often they hear the same kind of input constantly and/or are in situations where they produce a great deal but do not actually hear or read much (e.g. a gas-station attendant).

48. See, however, the discussion of vocabulary acquisition later in this chapter.

49. From Yorkey et. al. Book II

50. See Krashen 1982a, Chapter Four.

51. From Neuner et. al., p. 91.

52. These figures vary greatly, of course, and depend on many factors, such as motivation, the relationship between native and target languages, and so forth.

53. Stevick's interesting review and discussion of memory studies in experimental psychology (Stevick, 1976; Chapters Two and Three) does not provide direct evidence, but is supportive of this view. No studies pit vocabulary acquisition via real communication against drill or exercise methods, but experiments do support the idea that meaningful, creative mental activity is necessary for items to enter permanent storage, especially when subjects are personally involved with the items to be retained ("depth", in Stevick's terms). It may be the case that genuine comprehensible input is the best way to achieve the necessary level of activity and involvement for real acquisition of vocabulary.

54. We should point out that this philosophy does not forbid the occasional use of the dictionary. It may be essential to look up a word at times in order to understand a text (see footnote 28, this chapter). Also, acquirers may occasionally need to ask native speakers for meanings of words, both in class and on the outside. This procedure may help acquisition of a word by making its next appearance more comprehensible. Its main function, however, is to make the current discourse more comprehensible. It need not lead to the acquisition of the particular lexical item.

55. There is no research we know of that tells us how many repetitions of a word in a comprehensible message are necessary for it to be acquired. This question, in fact, may not be answerable in an obvious way. Stevick (1982; see also Chapters Two and Three in Stevick, 1976) suggests that for true acquisition, frequency may play no role at all; only "intensity," personal relevance or "depth" may be important. (See footnote 53, this chapter.) A highly "intense" word may be acquired after only one exposure (Stevick 1982, p. 31). Frequency, on the other hand, may be relevant for short-term retention.

Chapter Seven

Testing and Classroom Management

TESTING

> The Role of Testing in the Natural Approach
> General Considerations
> Listening Comprehension
> Speaking
> Reading and Writing
> Vocabulary Tests

ORDER OF GRAMMAR RULES

ERROR CORRECTION

MODIFICATION FOR AGE DIFFERENCES

MODIFICATION FOR SECOND LANGUAGE INSTRUCTION

TESTING

The Role of Testing in the Natural Approach

Evaluating student progress is a necessity in academic situations and can even be a useful part of the curriculum. Before outlining some general considerations on testing within the framework on the N.A., we must first look briefly at some possible theoretical problems.

The core of the N.A. is language acquisition. As we explained in Chapter Two, language acquisition is a subconscious process, dependent on two factors: the amount of comprehensible input the students get, and the strength of their affective filters, that is the amount of input the students "allow in". It is, thus, in a sense, unfair to grade students on the amount of target language they acquire since it is up to the instructor to provide the input, at least in class, and since the strength of the filter is beyond their conscious control. Rather, it could be argued that we should only grade on factors such as attendance and participation. In addition, although it is relatively simple to construct "discrete point" tests, tests that focus on one grammatical point or vocabulary item at a time, it is more difficult to construct and evaluate tests that tap a student's ability to use the language in communicative situations.

Despite these difficulties, it may be possible to test in a way that is not unfair, and that is reasonably valid. Moreover, it can be done in a way that will have a positive effect on the student's progress. The key to effective testing is the realization that testing has a profound effect on what goes on in the classroom. Teachers are motivated to teach, and students are motivated to study, material which will be covered on tests. Quite simply, if we want students to acquire a second language, we should give tests that promote the use of acquisition activities. In other words, our tests should motivate students to prepare for the tests by obtaining more comprehensible input and motivate teachers to supply it. Using an approach in the classroom which emphasizes the ability to exchange messages and at the same time testing only the ability to apply grammar rules correctly, is an invitation to a disaster.

In the following sections we will provide some suggestions and guidelines for testing. We do not have perfect answers. Short of following students around and eavesdropping on their conversation with native speakers (if, indeed, they are available), there is no perfect way to test communication skills. We will suggest tests which try to maintain the focus on message receiving and giving while taking into account the realities of the demands on the instructor and the possibilities of the classroom setting.

General Considerations

Carroll lists four criteria for judging the merits of a particular test: relevance, acceptability, comparability and economy. [1] By relevance, Carroll refers to whether the test actually measures the communication skills the students need.

For us, relevance underscores the necessity to coordinate what is tested directly with the goals of the course. For example, if the goal is simply to translate short passages from one language to another, then translation tests are appropriate. On the other hand, if the goal is to be able to participate in normal conversation about current events with a native speaker, it is difficult to see how a translation test could measure this ability since the salient characteristic of such interchanges is that translation is virtually impossible. If one of the goals of a course is to develop the ability to comprehend radio weather forecasts, then such broadcasts can be recorded and the students tested to ascertain whether they can understand the information.

By acceptability, Carroll refers to the willingness of the students to participate in the testing and their satisfaction that the test does indeed evaluate their progress. A test by its very nature will create a certain amount of strain and nervousness. This tension can be beneficial at times, but for many students it simply prevents them from performing according to their competence. Acceptability can be increased by making sure that the format of the test is well understood, by allowing the students to become familiar with tests with similar or identical format, by making the content of the test relevant to the goals of the course and to the sorts of activities which have taken place in class.

By comparability, Carroll refers to the possibility of being able to compare test scores of different groups of students or of the same group of students at different times. Comparability is a complex issue and it is doubtful that tests written by the instructor (as opposed to standardized tests) will rank high in comparability. But, at least some effort should be made so that in classes with the same goals, the students' evaluations are at least minimally comparable across classes and across instructors. On the other hand, if the goals of different courses are radically different, then comparability is neither necessary nor particularly desirable.

By economy, Carroll means the possibility of obtaining a relatively large amount of information in a short period of time and without an inordinate amount of energy expended by the instructor and students. For example, a moderately long oral interview is a relatively good measure of oral communication fluency. On the other hand, for an instructor with 30 or more students in a class, interview testing requires an enormous amount of time and energy. And if the interviews must be conducted in class time, it is difficult to avoid allowing the other students to waste their time while the instructor interviews each individual student. In the case of the instructor with five or six classes per day with 30 or more students, not an uncommon arrangement, economy of the oral exam becomes a paramount consideration.

Language proficiency tests can be classified as tests of **linguistic competence** or **communicative competence.** By linguistic competence, we refer to the ability to control pronunciation, morphology, and syntax; by communicative competence, we mean the ability to use language to achieve a particular purpose. It is clear that while the two competencies are related, they are not interchangeable. There are all too many examples of students who, through the study of grammar, have achieved a relatively high level of linguistic competence, but, who, in real communicative situations, cannot exchange much information at all. Our goal is for students to achieve both communicative and linguistic competence. The main thrust of the Natural Approach is that one should first aim for communicative competence; significant grammatical competence will follow. We are thus not sacrificing accuracy for fluency. Rather, a focus on communicative facility entails greater participation in real communication, which in turn entails more comprehensible input, resulting in greater acquisition of grammar. Thus, it follows that in beginning stages we prefer tests that evaluate the students' ability to understand and communicate ideas in specific situations, rather than tests of pronunciation, morphology and syntax. What is required is that the goals of the course specify the degree of both communicative and linguistic competence which will be expected of students. Our feeling is that in many, perhaps most, beginning language courses, linguistic goals are set at an impossibly high level for the average student, while communicative goals are so minimal as to be in many (most?) cases non-existent. Thus, in the sections which follow, we will discuss ways to test communication skills: Descriptions of grammar tests will be conspicuously absent. When linguistic goals are set too high, we see neither linguistic nor communicative competence. When communicative goals are emphasized, we see both.

Tests may be either situational or abstract. By abstract, we mean that the item being tested has no direct, immediate base in the student's reality. Communicative tests by their very nature are not abstract, although students should not be asked to communicate about unfamiliar topics and/or in unfamiliar situations. On the other hand, tests of linguistic competence are often entirely abstract. Students may be asked to transform sentences which are completely out of context and have no real referent. For example, "Change the following sentence to the past tense: *John goes to the store.* Who is John? What store? When? Why? To complete such a task, we must think about language not as a tool for the communication of ideas, but as an abstract entity which can be manipulated by following certain rules.

On the other hand, contextualizing a grammar test, i.e., a test of linguistic competence, while an improvement, does not change it into a test of communication skills. Suppose that the above example appeared in the following context: *"My cousin's name is John Baker. Last night about 8 o'clock he disappeared. My mother asked, 'Where did John go?' I think that he _____ to the store, I replied."* While it is possible that the student will understand the meaning and fill in the blank on the basis of acquired knowledge, it is also possible that the student will simply figure out the morphological pattern and change *go* to *went* without even understanding the text. In a real test of communication skills this sort of avoidance is impossible because of the very nature of the exam.

Finally, we refer to exams as either **global** or **discrete point.** By discrete point we mean that separate items are tested. Usually, tests of linguistic competence are discrete point tests. [2] For example, we may have a paragraph which is written in the present tense and must be rewritten by the student in the past tense. Each verb change is a discrete item which is either correct or incorrect. Global exams, on the other hand, try to measure a general language ability or at least several sorts of competencies. For example, students may be asked to listen to a news broadcast and list seven important events. Or, on an oral exam, the students may be asked to recount a scary experience from their lives. Discrete point tests are relatively simple to score, while global exams may present more difficulties.

Exams may be single focus or mixed mode.[3] Single focus tests concentrate on a single skill at a time, for example the ability to comprehend spoken language in a certain context. Mixed mode tests evaluate several skills at once. For example, the oral interview requires the ability to comprehend the questions and comments of the interviewer as well as respond to them. The use of single or mixed mode exams depends on various factors: the goals of the course, the setting of the exam, and particularly the time available.

In the following sections we will suggest some ways of testing which, although not without flaws, may be of use to instructors who use Natural Approach techniques or who try to emphasize communication skills.

Listening Comprehension

Usually the ability to understand spoken language is used in conjunction with other skills: in a normal conversation we use both listening and speaking skills. There are, however, occasions in which we must use primarily listening skills and even in case of multi-mode use of skills, we may wish to test listening comprehension skills separately for other reasons, e.g., ease of testing.

In the Natural Approach, the testing of the ability to comprehend speech takes on a singular importance since the Natural Approach is based on the mechanism of acquisition through comprehensible input.

In the prespeaking stage, testing of listening comprehension may seem to amount to no more than an examination of the ability to recognize vocabulary. This is only superficially true. What we really wish to test is the developing ability to recognize key lexical items and to use context to guess at meaning. Such tests are relatively simple to construct using pictures of various people, items and situations. One of the easiest techniques is to present students with various pictures and then describe one of the pictures, asking the students to identify the one being described. In this sort of test, care must be taken so that the description is neither too simple (identification by a single word) nor too complex (identification only possible if the students hear a particular word or morpheme).

Another relatively simple technique is to make statements about pictures, items, or actions and ask the students to judge whether they are true or false. For example, holding up a picture of a man and a woman horseback riding, the instructor might say, *There are three people in this picture. The man is on the right side of the woman. They are both riding the same horse.* Or, using props brought to class, the instructor can perform certain actions and then ask about them: *First, I took the napkin and placed it on the table, and then I laid the spoon on top of it.*

The ball is in front of the book, but the eraser is behind it.

As students develop into the single word stage, they can be asked simple questions, again using pictures or some other context: *What color is the little girl's hat? How many people are in the picture? What do you see in back of the tree?* Note that our goal is to test comprehension of the question, not whether the student knows the word to express the answer. Thus, the vocabulary used in the answer should be well known by all the students, and the only issue is whether they understand the question or statement.[4]

As students begin to produce sentences and engage in discourse, more sophisticated tests of listening comprehension are necessary. Let us first consider examples of the sorts of listening activities which might logically form a part of many language courses: (1) listening in on a conversation, (2) participating in a conversation, (3) receiving an oral message (e.g. on the telephone), (4) listening to an extended oral narrative (story, joke, etc.), (5) listening to instructions (how to), (6) listening to radio broadcasts (news, special programs), (7) songs, (8) television shows of all sorts, (9) commercials (radio and TV), (10) a lecture, (11) a movie. This list is, of course, suggestive, not exhaustive.

Skills 1-5 are probably required of all who expect to participate even minimally in another culture. Skills 9-11 are more specialized and many students of a second language never attain this level of comprehension.

Skill 1, listening in on a conversation, is relatively easy to test although there are some difficulties with the format. The instructor, preferably using native speakers, records a dialog in which the situation and topics are relevant to the students' communication goals in the course. The students listen to the dialog one or more times and then answer questions about the content of the dialog. In order to encourage global listening, the questions should be somewhat general, avoiding details.

There are some problems with using recorded dialogs as tests that instructors should be aware of. A recorded dialog and a real conversation can be quite different. The live version will have gestures, facial expressions, and other body language to help comprehension. In addition, recorded, prewritten dialogs are really examples of written language, not spoken language, since many aspects of real speech which help us comprehend are missing. These include false starts, pauses, repetitions, asides, explanations *(I mean)*, pause holders *(you know)* and so forth. On the other hand, conversation which includes these traits, if only heard as a recording and not in person, is quite difficult to understand. The optimal solution, where possible, would be to have a real conversation between two or more native speakers in front of the class. A video tape of a real conversation helps alleviate some, but not all, of the problems of a prerecorded dialog.

Care must be taken with the form and placing of the questions. We prefer to give questions to the students first so that they have some idea of the information they are looking for before they hear the dialog. If questions are given after the students hear the dialog, the test may become one of memory, more than of comprehension.

Skill 2, participating in a conversation, is the goal of most language students and can be tested directly in an interview situation. There are certain pitfalls we would like to avoid with this kind of test. Testers sometimes tend to ask questions with the students always answering. While the ability to understand questions is one we are certainly interested in, in normal conversations there is a wide variety of interactions which the students must comprehend, such as comments, commands, requests, exclamations, rhetorical questions, and so forth, all of which should be included in a good interview test.[5]

Skills 3-5, listening to messages of various sorts, are easily tested since no interaction between dialog participants is necessary. The simplest technique is for the instructor to narrate a story, or convey information or instructions to the class and subsequently use questions to determine how much they have understood. For the same reasons as mentioned above, we prefer that the students be given the questions before they receive the oral input. If it is desirable to avoid a multi-mode test, the questions can be of the true-false form.

Skills 6-11, listening to radio, TV, songs, movies, etc. may be tested directly by using the appropriate media and essentially the same techniques mentioned above.

Before leaving this section, we will comment on certain techniques now common in testing listening comprehension. Most of these techniques were inherited from the audiolingual era. The most common is to present the student with a sentence followed by a series of responses (both stimulus and possible responses are presented orally). The student chooses the correct response.

It's hot today.	*J'ai faim.*
a. *Good, let's go to the beach.*	a. *Allons étudier.*
b. *I'm studying mathematics.*	b. *Allons manger.*
c. *Joan is my sister.*	c. *Allons écrire une lettre.*

This particular technique, while easy to administer and to evaluate, is extremely artificial. We normally do not hear language as a series of unrelated and out-of-context statements, followed by even more unrelated responses. The task of the student listener on these exams is much greater than in real life communicative situations. Nor is there any way the student can directly study for such an exam by engaging in oral communication.

Whatever technique is used to evaluate listening comprehension it should meet the requirement that student preparation in and of itself aids acquisition. If, for example, the students are aware of the fact that an exam will be taken from TV or radio, they will spend time listening to radio and watching television in the target language. This, in itself, will help acquisition since it means more comprehensible input. If, on the other hand, test preparation forces the student away from activities that bring in comprehensible input, the test may be counter-productive.

We recognize that the testing of the ability to comprehend speech is not easy logistically. It demands a greater investment of time and effort than a simple grammar test. However, it is essential to test listening comprehension in some form if one of the goals of the course is that the student be able to extract information from the language spoken.

Speaking

As in the case of listening comprehension, speech production is a skill rarely used in an isolated fashion but rather is combined with other skills, normally comprehension in a dialog situation. There are a good number of techniques for evaluating the ability to communicate ideas by means of speech. None, except for perhaps following students around and listening to their conversations with native speakers, are perfect measures of communications skills.

Interestingly enough, in spite of the fact that speech is a goal in most language courses, the ability to speak the language being studied is not tested directly in many cases. It is too often simply assumed that if the students can do well on grammar tests, then they will also be able to speak. Or, there may be a great deal of time devoted to developing oral communication skills in the classroom, but evaluation is then completely in a written mode. The main reason for the avoidance of oral tests of speech production is lack of time: it takes a great deal of time to give an oral test to five or six classes of 25-35 students. Added to the problem of time is one of grading: how does one objectively grade oral production without resorting to some simplistic scale of grammatical and phonological correctness?

It is certainly true that it takes more time to administer oral exams to a large group of students than commonly used discrete-point grammar exams. On the other hand, it is possible to build such exams into the curriculum without major disruptions. One technique is to spread the exams out over several days, so that while the instructor is working with one or several students, the others are busy with other sorts of activities. Another is to designate a special day for oral exams. If tape recorders are available, then more than one student can take the exam at a time.

Let us consider briefly the problem of grading an oral exam. Do we wish to grade students simply on their overall fluency and their ability to exchange information, or do we want to do a detailed analysis of their output? Do we want to utilize the impressions of judges or rely on more "careful" analyses?

Let us deal with the second question first. There is good evidence that impressionistic ratings, while they seem to be very subjective, can be made quite reliable. The Foreign Service Exam, perhaps the best known oral test in the United States, uses this method; in the FSI, students are engaged by a trained interviewer in a loosely-structured conversation for 10 to 20 minutes. Ratings are made by judges, but criteria for ratings are quite precise and trainers are trained to insure that the criteria are applied consistently from one tester to another. [6]

There is also evidence that rating each component separately may not be necessary. Oller (1979) maintains, on the basis of studies by Callaway (1980) and Mullen (1980), that subjective ratings by judges "always seem to be evaluating communicative effectiveness, regardless of whether they are trying to gauge 'fluency', 'accentedness', 'nativeness', 'grammar', 'vocabulary', 'content', 'comprehension', or whatever." (p. 392). Oller concludes that subjective ratings that aim at communicative effectiveness "are about as informative as objective scores in terms of differentiating between better and worse performances of the individuals in a group of students." (p. 394).

One advantage of evaluating oral exams for beginning students only on fluency and the ability to communicate ideas is that this encourages the "right" sort of test preparation. The best way to study for the tests is by participating in conversation! If they do this, they will gain more input, and if they obtain more input, they will acquire more.

Let us now turn to a closer look at possible ways to test specific speaking skills. There are several readily identifiable skills of speech production: (1) speech in a conversational interchange, (2) narrating, telling jokes, recounting events, giving instructions, (3) formal talks or speeches (class reports, panels, etc.), (4) debates, arguments. This list is meant to be only suggestive.

Skill 1, speech in a conversational interchange, is probably the most useful and basic for beginning language students since it will be needed in almost any contact with native speakers. It is also perhaps the most difficult to test since it is almost impossible to set up a real conversational situation in the classroom. Added to this is the difficulty of providing a chance for individual students to participate in an interchange which demonstrates their communicative competence. There are several techniques which have been used successfully (although keep in mind that all have certain drawbacks). The most widely used of oral exams is the oral interview (of which the FSI exam is the best known, as we have mentioned) in which the instructor (or a native speaker) asks open-ended questions in a "relaxed" (as much as possible) informal context, trying to stimulate as much conversational output from the student as possible. In a classroom situation the interview-exam must naturally be limited to the topics and situations the student has been dealing with.

Another technique is to pair the students and ask them to engage in a conversation which can be evaluated by listening directly to the conversation or later to a recording of the conversation. This later technique has the advantage that if several recorders are available, many more students can take the test at the same time. Also, the evaluation of taped conversations (or interviews) can be more objective since the speech of one student can be listened to several times and even compared directly to that of other students.

Tests of Skill 2, narration, are easier logistically since the students can narrate without needing a partner to contribute. Narrations are also easy to record for later evaluation. Tests of Skills in 3, formal speech, and 4, debates, are also relatively easy to set up since they can be a part of the class activities which are evaluated by the instructor as the activity takes place.

Reading and Writing

Tests of reading and writing will be of use in courses for which reading and writing skills are goals. This is true of college preparatory ESL classes, for example, but often is not true of adult foreign language "travel" courses in which the students mainly want to learn how to "get by" in another culture. Whether reading and writing exams are given in Natural Approach classes depends entirely on the goals and needs of the students.

Recall first that a test of reading is not the same as a test of translation abilities nor is a test of writing simply a grammar test. Reading skills, as we noted in Chapter Six, are varied. It is not the same to skim a news article as to read a personal letter; nor is the perusal of an advertisement in a newspaper the same as reading a chemistry assignment for a college course. And, of course, none of these is the same as the reading of prose for enjoyment. Thus, the what and how of the testing of reading depends naturally on what the students need to learn how to read. Let us consider the testing of the following texts as examples: (1) forms, signs and advertisements, (2) newspapers and general interest nonfiction, (3) pleasure reading of fiction, (4) academic reading and study.

For type (1) we would select forms, signs or advertisements from the target language and ask questions which test the students' comprehension. For type (2), newspaper and general interest reading, and (3), pleasure reading, the standard tests used to evaluate reading skills in our native language are useful in adapted form. Usually in these tests the students read a passage (which is complete and coherent even out of a larger context) and answer questions on the passage. Normally, these questions require some sort of inferencing. In (1), (2), and (3) the student will often make use of scanning and skimming skills. On the contrary, in testing the ability to read academic material, (4), we want the students to concentrate on a close reading of the passage.

A well-constructed test of reading comprehension, i.e., one that tests readers on whether they have understood the main point, or "gist" of the text, and one that provides a variety of topics, easily meets the requirement that a test have a beneficial effect on student behavior. There is only one way to study for such a reading comprehension test: read! And if they read, they will acquire!

As with reading, writing is a skill which is not relevant to all students in all language courses. In many language courses, students are required to produce essays written in a second language or do long complex translations, when, in fact, they will never use these skills after they finish the course. In other courses, such as college preparatory language courses, such skills may be more relevant.

The testing of writing depends, then, on the writing tasks which are considered to be goals in the course. Sample tasks are: (1) filling out forms, (2) writing personal letters, (3) writing business letters, (4) writing personal narratives, (5) writing essays, (6) writing fiction or poetry.

The administration of writing tests is straightforward. There are a variety of techniques available that generate student prose in a second language. Possibilities range from simple description to essays on topics of general concern or personal interest. As is the case with the evaluation of speech, evaluating writing is complex.

Writing samples may be evaluated in several ways. First, we may attempt to look at students' writing as an indication of what they have acquired. Using writing instead of speech has a definite advantage for the tester; while speech samples must be tape-recorded or transcribed, or necessitate a one-on-one student tester dyad, writing samples are easily stored and can be graded at home at leisure. There are, however, problems. First, as we mentioned in discussing grading speech output, there is the question of whether we are looking for grammatical accuracy or the ability to transmit information, or both. Second, and more seriously, using writing as a measure of acquisition does not have a positive effect on student behavior. If it is true that acquisition comes from input, and not output, students will have to be told that they can "practice" for the writing test by reading and listening.

Another way of evaluating writing is to judge it as a measure of Monitor efficiency. There is some justification in this, as effective Monitor use is a desirable goal as part of the curriculum. Also, there could be positive effects on student behavior. If students know in advance that they will be writing, and that their writing will be graded only on grammatical accuracy for rules that they have studied, we can expect some beneficial practice of this skill. There are dangers, however. One chance, discussed in the "grammar" section, is that the monitoring function will become overemphasized at beginning stages. We thus recommend that writing as a test of learning not be used at beginning levels. Another problem is the tendency to judge students on all errors. Since the use of the Monitor is limited, as discussed in Chapter Two, we should only expect monitoring to have an effect on a limited number of rules. Because of these considerations, we suggest not relying on writing output as a test in the elementary levels of foreign language classes.

ORDER OF GRAMMAR RULES

In most grammar-based approaches in common use today (grammar-translation, audiolingual, and cognitive), grammatical rules are presented as a system to be learned in discrete steps. The structure or form (for example, a verb conjugation, a rule of agreement, a set of exceptions, etc.) is presented by explanation. Then, students are given a series of exercises or drills with minimal semantic content to focus them on the correct form of the rule in question. Finally, after a "suitable" amount of practice, the instructor encourages students to attempt to apply the rule in more or less real conversation. (Usually "less" since the conversation is forced into strange twists in order to maintain the focus on application of the rule.) At the end of a unit (which may comprise several grammar rules), the students are tested on their knowledge of the rule. During the course, experienced instructors build in review and reentry mechanisms. However, virtually all courses follow this building block concept — introduction, explanation, practice, application, testing. The cycle is applied then again to a new structure or set of forms. The following figure is a schematic representation of such a model for order and sequencing of certain grammatical morphemes for a beginning Spanish course.

FIGURE ONE
Learning of Structure in Grammar

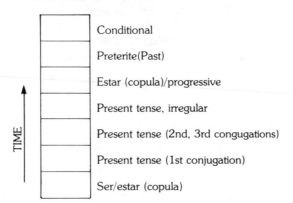

TIME

Conditional

Preterite(Past)

Estar (copula)/progressive

Present tense, irregular

Present tense (2nd, 3rd conjugations)

Present tense (1st conjugation)

Ser/estar (copula)

While this may be a reasonable model for second language learning, it is totally divorced from what we know about order of acquisition of grammar.

In Chapter Two we discussed research on the order of acquisition of morphemes for various groups of acquirers. It might be thought that it would be advisable to sequence the introduction of rules into the activities according to the natural order of acquisition. As discussed earlier, this proposal faces several difficulties, the most serious being that it seriously interferes with communication—when our "hidden agenda" is the presentation of a grammatical rule, it is very hard to focus on meaing. If the Input Hypothesis is correct, on the other hand, providing comprehensible input in sufficient quantity will automatically deliver the right grammar; $i+1$ will automatically be present. Thus, one needs only to create a syllabus based on communicative goals and sequencing of grammatical rules will take care of itself. The arguments against a grammatical syllabus and the arguments for a communicative syllabus hold even if the grammatical syllabus under discussion is a "natural" one!

There is another sense in which we should examine the notion of order of sequence in the acquisition process. To this point, we have referred to the acquisition of rules as if it were an instantaneous process, i.e., a certain rule or sub-rule is acquired at a certain point in time. Instructors used to grammar-based discrete level teaching as illustrated in Figure 1 may ask when in a N.A. course the subjunctive mood is acquired. Instructors of a Romance language may wish to know when the students acquire the difference between the perfective past and the imperfect past; teachers of German may want to know when the Dative case endings are acquired. These questions are asked because we are used to viewing these matters in terms of the entire system, i.e., subjunctive mood, imperfect tense functions, case in nouns, and so forth. It is quite improbable that these rule systems are acquired as a unit; rather they are most probably acquired piece by piece, by subparts until the whole system is acquired.

For the acquisition of grammar in a second language classroom, we envision a sort of horizontal acquisition scheme in which the students start and finish specific parts of sub-rules at different times and at different rates. In the following figure, we give a hypothetical illustration from Spanish.

FIGURE TWO
Acquisition of structure in the N.A.

TIME

1 2 3 4 5 6 7 8 9 10

Pres. tense
3rd sing.

Pres. tense
1st sing.

Pres. tense
1st pl.

Pres. tense
3rd pl.

Ser
(with nouns)

Estar
(sith gerunds)

Past (preterite)
1st sing.

Conditional
(all pers. numb.)

It is not our goal in this section to recommend a different grammatical syllabus, one based less on paradigm and more on subparts of rules. As we have maintained earlier, there are serious problems with any grammatical syllabus in terms of acquisition. We present this alternative view of order of acquisition in an attempt to alert teachers to what they can expect in their students' output. Not only will errors be plentiful, expecially in early stages and in Monitor-free performance, but teachers can also expect acquisition to proceed in this way, piece by piece, with parts of tenses and paradigms overlapping. This sort of sequence, we maintain, is not a matter of worry, but a sign that natural language acquisition is taking place.

In summary then, the only firm sequence we recommend is one based on communication goals. This means a semantic orientation rather than a linguistic one, i.e., should a student learn to order a meal in a restaurant or learn how to talk about previous vacations first? In any case, which will come first will be determined on the basis of which is more comprehensible and which one is more relevant to the students.

ERROR CORRECTION

The correction of speech errors plays a major role in most language courses. This is not surprising since, as we have repeatedly pointed out, for the most part these courses are aimed at the creation of language knowledge primarily through learning rather than acquisition. In these courses, the principal way of internalizing knowledge about the rules of the language is through explanation and practice with cognitive grammar exercises or audiolingual drills. In both cases, the correction of errors, either in speech or in written work, is intended to help the students adjust their conscious mental picture of the rule.

On the other hand, since the N.A. is primarily based on acquisition activities in the class period, it is necessary to consider whether the direct correction of speech errors in these activities is beneficial or detrimental. Our view is that overt error correction of speech even in the best of circumstances is likely to have a negative effect on the students' willingness to try to express themselves. Thus, the question is whether or not the possible positive effects of the correction of speech errors outweigh the intrinsic negative effects with regard to raising the affective filter.

The direct correction of speech errors appears to have almost no effect on first language and child second language acquisition. In reality, parents and other caretakers of children do very little direct correction of speech. In Chapter Two, we discussed the finding that caretakers correct only a very small fraction of the child's errors and that for the most part even this correction usually involves the appropriateness of what the child has said rather than the specific grammar rules the child has violated. It was also pointed out that this correction seems to have little or no effect on the direction and subsequent development of the child's system of grammar rules.

This appears also to be the case for adult second language acquirers. [7] For the most part, other adults refrain from correcting the grammatical mistakes of a non-native. What caretakers and foreigners do, of course, is to try to understand the intent of the non-native speaker and reply appropriately. Thus, if the non-native has produced an utterance which is incomprehensible, the native adult or the caretaker of children will attempt to make sense of what he or she has heard. This may take the form of a reformulated question, of using some of the non-native's words in a possible sentence, or simply restating what he believes the non-native has said. If the mistakes were of a minor sort in terms of comprehension, the native for the most part will simply reply appropriately, sometimes with a reformulation to check the non-native's intent. For example, if a student of Spanish were to say, ¿ Hablan usted inglés? in which the verb form signals plurality and the pronoun is you-singular, the native will either assume the student's pronoun choice was correct and ignore the verb mistake or he may ask a ques-like, ¿Si yo hablo inglés? 'Do I speak English?' to verify the non-native's intent.

In N.A. class activities, since the intent of the activity is to create the opportunity for conversational exchange which is as natural as possible, the instructor will unconsciously and automatically use these sorts of reformulations and expansions, just as in real-life situations. It is not clear that this sort of expansion is actually responsible for encouraging the students to speak more accurately and correctly. It is more likely that although some students do use this direct natural feedback for conscious inductive learning, the main contribution of the instructor's expansion is that it provides more comprehensible input. In fact, it may well be that the most usable input received by the student is in an exchange in which the instructor is trying, by expansion, to understand the meaning of what the student has incorrectly said.

Thus, our theoretical perspective as well as empirical research back up the N.A.'s principle of not using direct correction of speech errors in affective acquisition activities. Error correction should be used for what it was meant for, conscious learning, and should therefore be limited to rules and situations where Monitoring is possible and appropriate.

MODIFICATION FOR AGE DIFFERENCES

The principles of the Natural Approach apply to language acquirers of all ages. Children, adolescents, and adults all utilize language acquisition as the primary means of developing competence in a second language. Thus, the input-rich acquisition-based classroom will, in principle, be suitable for all students of all ages.

As we indicated earlier, among acquirers of all ages there are some differences that need to be considered. First, the topics of the acquisition activities need to be different for students of different ages. For younger students, for example, there may be greater emphasis on providing input via games and physical response activities.

A second difference mentioned in Chapter Two, is that younger acquirers will tend to have less ability and/or inclination to learn conscious rules. The amount of homework devoted to conscious learning might therefore vary according to age, with adults receiving the most, teenagers somewhat less, and children perhaps none at all. (However, recall that even a large subset of adults, under-users of the Monitor, will also profit little, if at all, from formal learning). Thus, a common mistake made in many language courses for children is giving students learning tasks similar to the grammar exercises used by adults. Grammar-based exercises used to develop the Monitor in adults are not effective for teaching children.

A third difference relates to attainment. The second language acquisition literature informs us that while adults may be faster in initial stages of second language acquisition, children are better in the long run (Krashen, Long and Scarcella, 1979). Younger acquirers also tend to exhibit a longer silent period. A serious problem is thus often created by trying to force production in children before a wide range of listening comprehension has been done.

Acquisition by adolescents merits special consideration. The affective filter in these years is extremely high for most individuals and peer evaluation is probably the single most important factor in the behavior of an adolescent. For this reason, it takes a very talented instructor to create an atmosphere favorable for acquisition among a group of young teenagers.

Older adults can also be successful in the language classroom if they are provided with the sort of acquisition-rich environments we have described. Exactly the same factors for acquisition are at work, although the instructor needs to use activities and situations specifically aimed at lowering the adults' affective filter. Typically, it takes more time for older adults to become acquainted with each other and to feel comfortable with others in the class. (For some suggestions see Stevick 1980, Moskovitz 1979).

MODIFICATION FOR SECOND LANGUAGE INSTRUCTION

The N.A. applies both to *foreign language* study, that is, to study of a language that is not spoken in the country of the student (e.g. French in the United States), as well as *second language* study, the study of a language that is spoken in the country (e.g. English as a second language in the United States). Despite some obvious differences between second and foreign language study, there is a fundamental similarity between them: both second and foreign languages need to be acquired if any reasonable level of achievement is expected, and in both cases language acquisition will occur via comprehensible input. The Natural Approach can supply this comprehensible input to both foreign and second language acquirers, input that may be unavailable outside the class in the case of students of a foreign language or may be difficult to obtain in the case of many students of a second language.

In parts of this text we have oriented the discussion to foreign language classrooms. In these classes, the advantages of the input-rich classroom are obvious. The classroom, in most cases, is practically the only source of comprehensible input in the target language. Less obvious is the fact that the classroom may be the only real source of comprehensible input for many second language acquirers as well. The student living in the culture where the language is spoken can easily obtain input in large quantities. Obtaining comprehensible input, on the other hand, may not be quite so simple. It is not always easy for beginning students at an extremely low level to put themselves into situations in which they interact with native speakers on a one-to-one basis. In fact, the reverse is often true: beginners often avoid placing themselves into situations in which they will be forced to interact in the target language simply because they can understand and say very little. Even those who have learned some of the target language and can manufacture some sentences using the L1 plus Monitor Mode (Chapter Two) find themselves having trouble understanding the responses to their attempts. When attempting to interact with rank beginners, it is often difficult for native speakers to reduce their speech to the correct level to provide comprehensible input, especially if they have had little contact with foreigners. If students can make contact and interact with native speakers over a period of time, assuming that the two have mutual interests, then the opportunity for comprehensible input increases, and native speakers are able to provide the input which the students need for acquisition.

The N.A. classroom, on the other hand, contains an instructor whose main purpose is to do just this — to create a net of speech which will enable students to begin interacting using the target language and to begin the acquisition process. There are other characteristics of the classroom which can lend themselves to the advantage of students in a second language acquisition situation: the instructor can provide a large amount of intake without forcing the students to respond in the target language immediately. Thus, students can benefit from hearing a large amount of understandable speech without being embarrassed with inadequate responses. Students in the classroom also have the advantage of being able to interact in meaningful situations with other students at or near their own level of competency. We referred to this earlier as interlanguage talk (Chapter Two). Just the presence of others at their level may provide a less threatening environment for early production.

Another important feature of the classroom is that the instructor is aware of the specific vocabulary needs of the students and can concentrate on appropriate and useful domains. This is not always true for beginners in the real world. Often speakers simply wish to initiate conversation and begin with whatever topic is at hand.

Thus, our conclusion is that while the real world can provide excellent input for intermediates or advanced acquirers, it also can be difficult to deal with, especially for beginners, and much time is lost hearing input which is too far above the students' current level. The classroom consisting of acquisition activities can be an excellent environment for these early acquisition needs and in some cases the optimal source even for students in a second language situation.

Second language situations may, however, motivate some changes in N.A. methodology. Specifically, in linguistically heterogeneous classes it will not be possible for students to use their native language for asking questions or for responses. They will need to respond in the target language from the start. This is not a serious shift in procedure, especially for the older student, since spontaneous production in foreign language classes using Natural Approach methodology occurs surprisingly soon.

In addition, in most second language situations there should be a somewhat greater emphasis on early production via routines and patterns. As we have noted, routines and patterns allow "early" production based not on acquired linguistic competence, but on simple memorization of whole phrases and parts of phrases. Such routines serve to help acquirers participate more successfully in conversations with more proficient speakers and meet early communicative needs in the target culture.

In the case of a second language student in the classroom, the instructor may serve as a coordinator of inside and outside the class activities so that one complements and helps the other. In other words, the purpose of the classroom instruction is to facilitate and encourage the students to interact with native speakers in the target language outside the classroom. The classroom acquisition activities will be directed to the immediate needs of the students: asking directions, ordering food, shopping, talking to a landlady, participating in sports, participating in other classes in the target language, and so forth. For example, the instructor may set up role playing for a visit to the post office and then assign students to go there and actually transact business which they report to the class the following day. In this way, the classroom serves to open various facets of the culture for more input and further acquisition.

Another responsibility of the classroom, especially in second language situations, is to teach students how to control conversations with a native speaker in order to insure continued comprehensible input. Many beginners are understandably shy about initiating conversation with a native speaker. And native speakers, in turn, often make an effort to help beginners feel comfortable in a conversation. The native speaker usually picks the topic of conversation and controls it by assuming the role of questioner while the student grapples with the difficulties of interpreting what the native speaker is saying and then with producing some sort of response. This sort of interchange puts the student at a severe disadvantage, since the continuation of the conversation depends crucially on understanding what the native speaker has asked. If, on the other hand, acquirers are encouraged to assume the initiative and to control the conversation to a certain extent (by asking questions, for example), they are in a better position to choose the topics of conversation and to direct the flow of communication to areas they can deal with more easily. If, for example, the students formulate a question, then presumably they have some sort of idea of the answers which might be produced. Even in the worst of cases, when the response is very difficult to understand, the student has at least an idea of what the native speaker might have said, and can respond with another appropriate question. Thus if the student is in charge, the conversation can continue, even if the student's competence level is rather low. A sustained interchange is good for the beginner's own self-confidence. The native speaker may be impressed with the student's ability to sustain the conversation and perhaps encouraged to further the interaction. (There is nothing more discouraging for a native speaker than to interact with a beginner who understands so little that any real communication is impossible.)

The classroom is perhaps the optimal place to teach such communication strategies. At an early level the student should be able to practice these strategies, asking questions and directing the conversation to topics he is familiar with. These will include how to hold one's place while thinking of a word (*just a moment, let's see, that is . . .*), how to interrupt, how to indicate that one has not understood, and how to request clarification, and repetition. [8]

Notes

1. Carroll 1980.
2. Discrete point tests are tests that focus attention on one point of grammar at a time, Oller 1979
3. Carroll 1980.
4. Since these questions require one-word answers (either orally or written), this test is technically a mixed-mode test. But if the answers are scored as simply right or wrong, only comprehension is tested.
5. An interview is, of course, also multi-mode since it is almost impossible in an interview to evaluate only what the student has understood. We return to a consideration of the interview exam in the section on the testing of speech.
6. See Oller 1979, pp. 320-326 for discussion of the FSI.
7. In a recent study, Cardelle and Corno (1981) examined the effect of various types of error correction on the written grammar homework of 80 college level students of Spanish as a foreign language. They reported that "constructive critical feedback," correction which included both criticism and praise, produced greater results than criticism alone, praise alone, or no feedback. Since the homework assignments, pre-tests and post-tests were essentially all discrete-point grammar tasks, this result confirms our prediction (see Chapter Two) that error correction can be of value for conscious learning. (For more discussion of the effect of error correction, see Krashen 1982a, pp. 116-119.)
8. for further discussion, see Scarcella and Higa 1982, Krashen 1982a, pp. 76-79.

BIBLIOGRAPHY

Anderson, J. 1976. **Psycholinguistic experiments in foreign language testing.** St. Lucia, Queensland, Australia: University of Queensland Press.

Asher, J. 1965. "The strategy of total physical response: an application to learning Russian," *International Review of Applied Linguistics* 3: 292-9.

—————. 1966. "The learning strategy of total physical response: a review," *Modern Language Journal* 50: 79-84.

—————. 1969. "The total physical response approach to second language learning," *Modern Language Journal* 53: 3-18.

—————. 1977. **Learning Another Language Through Actions: The Complete Teacher's Guide.** Los Gatos, California: Sky Oaks Publications.

—————. 1979. "Motivating children and adults to acquire a second language," *SPEAQ Journal* 3 (no. 3-4): 87-99.

————— and R. Garcia. 1969. "The optimal age to learn a foreign language," *Modern Language Journal* 8: 334-41.

————— and B. Price. 1967. "The learning strategy of Total Physical Response: some age differences," *Child Development* 38: 1219-1227.

—————, J. Kusudo and R. de la Torre. 1974. "Learning a second language through commands: the second field test," *Modern Language Journal* 58 (no. 102): 24-32.

Balhsen, L. 1905. **The Teaching of Modern Languages.** (Translated by M. Blackmore Evans). Boston, Massachusetts: Ginn.

Bancroft, J. 1978. "The Lozanov method and its American adaptations," *Modern Language Journal* 62 (no. 4): 167-74.

Been, S. 1975. "Reading in the foreign language teaching program," *TESOL Quarterly* 9: 233-42.

Bialystok, E. 1978. "A theoretical model of second language learning," *Language Learning* 28: 69-83.

—————. 1979. "Explicit and implicit judgements of grammaticality." *Language Learning* 29: 81-103.

—————. 1979. "An analytical view of second language competence: a model and some evidence," *Modern Language Journal* 63 (no. 5-6): 257-62.

—————. 1979. "The role of conscious strategies in second language proficiency," *The Canadian Modern Language Review* 35: 372-94.

————— and M. Frohlich. 1977. "Aspects of second language learning in classroom settings," *Working Papers on Bilingualism* 13: 1-26.

—————. 1978. "The aural grammar test: description and implications," *Working Papers on Bilingualism* 15: 15-35.

—————. 1978. "Variables of classroom achievement in second language learning," *Modern Language Journal* 62: 327-35.

Bloom, L. 1970. **Language Development: Form and Function in Emerging Grammars.** Cambridge, Massachusetts: MIT Press.

Bolinger, D., et. al. 1969. **Modern Spanish.** New York: Harcourt, Brace and World.

Brooks, N. 1964. **Language and Language Learning.** New York: Harcourt, Brace and World.

Brown, R. 1973. **A First Language.** Cambridge, Massachusetts: Harvard University Press.

————— and C. Hanlon. 1970. "Derivational complexity and order of acquisition in child speech," **Cognition and the Development of Language,** ed., J. Hayes. New York:

Wiley and Sons, 155-207.

_____, C. Cazden and U. Bellugi. 1973. "The child's grammar from I to III," **Studies in Child Language Development,** eds., C. Ferguson and D. Slobin. New York: Holt, Rinehart, and Winston.

Buchanan, M. and E. MacPhee. 1928. **Modern Language Instruction in Canada.** Toronto, Canada: University of Toronto Press.

Cancino, H., E. Rosansky and J. Schuman. 1975. "The acquisition of the English auxiliary by native Spanish speakers," *TESOL Quarterly* 9: 421-30.

Cardelle, M. and L. Corno. 1981. "Effects on second language learning of variations in written feedback on homework assignments," *TESOL Quarterly* 15: 251-61.

Carroll, J. 1973. "Implications of aptitute test research and psycholinguistic theory of foreign language testing," *Linguistics* 112: 5-13.

_____. 1980. "Foreign language testing: persistent problems," **Readings on English as a Second Language,** ed. K. Croft. Cambridge, Massachusetts: Winthrop, 518-30.

Castro, O. and Kimbrough, V. 1980. **In Touch.** New York: Longman.

Cates, G. and J. Swaffer. 1979. **Reading in a Second Language.** Washington, D.C.: Center for Applied Linguistics (Language in Education Series, no. 20).

Chastain, K. 1976. **Developing Second Language Skills: Theory and Practice.** Chicago: Rand McNally College Publishing.

Christison, M. 1979. "Natural sequencing in adult second language acquisition," *TESOL Quarterly* 13: 122.

_____ and S. Bassano. 1981. **Look Who's Talking.** San Francisco, California: Alemany Press.

Clark, H. and E. Clark. 1977. **Psychology and Language.** New York: Harcourt, Brace and Jovanovich.

Clark, M. and S. Silberstein. 1977. "Toward a realization of psycholinguistic principles in the ESL reading class," *Language Learning* 27: 135-54.

Clark, R. 1974. "Performing without competence," *Journal of Child Language* 1:1-10.

Cohen, A., H. Glassman, R. Rosenbaum-Cohen, P. Ferrara, and J. Fine. 1979. "Reading English for specialized purposes: discourse analysis and the use of student informants," *TESOL Quarterly* 13: 551-64.

_____ and M. Robbins. 1976. "Towards assessing interlanguage performance: the relationship between selected errors, learner's characteristics and learner's explanations," *Language Learning* 26: 45-66.

Cole, R. 1931. **Modern Foreign Languages and their Teaching.** New York: Appleton-Century-Crofts.

Coleman, A. 1929. **The Teaching of Modern Foreign Languages in the United States.** New York: Macmillan Company.

Corder, S. 1967. "The significance of learner's errors," *International Journal of Applied Linguistics* 5: 161-70.

Cross, T. 1977. "Mother's speech adjustments," **Talking to Children,** eds., C. Snow and C. Ferguson. New York: Cambridge University Press, 151-88.

Cummins, J. 1980. "The cross-lingual dimensions of language proficiency: Implications for bilingual education and the optimal age issue," *TESOL Quarterly* 14: 175-187.

_____. 1981. "The role of primary language development in promoting educational success for language minority students," **Schooling and Language Minority Students: A Theoretical Framework,** State of California, Office of Bilingual Bicultural Education,

Los Angeles, California: California State University at Los Angeles, Evaluation, Dissemination and Assessment Center, 3-49.

Curran, C. 1976. **Counseling-Learning in Second Languages.** Apple River, Wisconsin: Apple River Press.

Cziko, G. 1978. "Differences in first and second language reading: the use of syntactic and discourse constraints," *The Canadian Modern Language Review* 34: 473-89.

d'Angeljan, A. and G. Tucker. 1975. "The acquisition of complex English structures by adult learners," *Language Learning* 25: 281-96.

DeSauzé, E. 1929. **The Cleveland Plan for the Teaching of Modern Languages.** Philadelphia, Pennsylvania: Winston Company.

deVilliers, J. and deVilliers. 1973. "A cross-sectional study of the acquisition of grammatical morphemes in child speech," *Journal of Psycholinguistic Research* 2: 267-78.

Diller, C. 1978. **The Language Teaching Controversy.** Rowley, Massachusetts: Newbury House.

Donaldson, D. 1922. "The direct method," *Hispania* 5: 360-4.

Dulay, H. and M. Burt. 1973. "Should we teach children syntax?" *Language Learning* 23 (no. 2): 245-58.

_____ . 1974. "Natural sequences in child second language acquisition," *Language Learning* 24: 37-53.

_____ . 1975. "A new approach to discovering universal strategies of child language acquisition," **Developmental Psycholinguistics: Theory and Applications,** ed., D. Dats. Washington, D.C.: Georgetown University School of Languages and Linguistics, 209-33.

_____ .1977. "Remarks on creativity in language acquisition," **Viewpoints on English as a Second Language,** eds. M. Burt, H. Dulay and M. Finocchiaro. New York: Regents, 95-126.

_____ : 1978. "Some guidelines for the assessment of oral language proficiency and dominance," *TESOL Quarterly* 12: 177-92.

Dulay, H., M. Burt, and S. Krashen, 1982. **Language Two.** New York: Oxford Press.

Elkind, D. 1967. "Egocentrism in adolescence," *Child Development* 38: 1025-34.

Ervin-Tripp, S. 1974. "Is second language learning like the first?," *TESOL Quarterly* 8: 111-27.

Fanselow, J. 1977. "The treatment of error in oral work," *Foreign Language Annals* 10 (no. 5): 583-93.

Freed, B. 1980. "Talking to children, talking to foreigners," Paper presented at the Second Language Research Forum, University of Southern California, Los Angeles, California.

Gaies, S. 1977. "The nature of linguistic input in formal second language learning," **On TESOL '77,** eds., H. Brown, C. Yorio and R. Crymes. Washington, D.C.: TESOL, 204-12.

Gardner, R. and W. Lambert. 1972. **Attitudes and Motivation in Second Language Learning.** Rowley, Massachusetts: Newbury House.

_____ , P. Smythe, R. Clement, and L. Gliksman, 1976. "Second language learning: a social-psychological perspective," *Canadian Modern Language Review* 32: 198-213.

Gary, J. and N. Gary. 1980. "Comprehension-oriented foreign language instruction: an overview," *The Linguistic Reporter* 23: 4-5.

Goodman, K. 1967. "Reading: a psycholinguistic guessing game," *Journal of the Reading Specialist* 6: 126-35.

_____ . 1971. "Psycholinguistic universals in the reading process," **The Psychology of Second Language Learning,** eds. P. Pimsleur and T. Quinn. Cambridge: University Press, 135-42.

_____ , Y. Goodman, and B. Flores, 1979. **Reading in the Bilingual Classroom:**

Literacy and Biliteracy. Rosslyn, Virginia: National Clearinghouse for Bilingual Education.

Grittner, F. 1977. **Teaching Foreign Languages.** New York: Harper and Row.

Gouin, F. 1980. **L'art d'enseigner et d'étudier les langues.** Paris: Librairie Fischbacher.

Hakuta, K. 1976. "Prefabricated patterns and the emergence of structure in second language acquisition," *Language Learning* 24: 287-98.

Hanania, E. and H. Gradman. 1977. "Acquisition of English structures: A case study of an adult native speaker in an English speaking environment," *Language Learning* 27: 75-92.

Hansen, J. 1981. "The effect of interference training and practice on young children's comprehension," *Reading Research Quarterly* 26: 391-417.

Hatch, E. 1974. "Research on reading a second language," *Journal of Reading Behavior* 6: 53-61.

_____ . 1979. "Reading a second language," **Teaching English as a Second or Foreign Language,** eds., M. Celce-Murcia and L. McIntosh. Rowley, Massachusetts: Newbury House.

_____ , B. Peck, and J. Wagner-Gough. 1979. "A look at process in child second-language acquisition," **Developmental Pragmatics,** eds., E. Ochs and B. Schieffelin. New York: Academic Press, 269-78.

_____ . R. Shapira and J. Gough. 1978. "Foreigner-talk discourse," *ITL: Review of Applied Linguistics* 39-40: 39-60.

Hauptman, P. 1981. "A comparison of first and second language reading strategies," *ITL: Review of Applied Linguistics* 51: 37-57.

_____ . 1982. "L'application d'une théorie cognitive à la lecture en langue seconde," *Champs Educatifs* 3.

Hawkins, J. 1978. **Definiteness and Indefiniteness: a Study of Reference and Grammaticality Prediction.** London: Croom-Helm Publishers.

Heyde, A. 1977. "The relationship between self-esteem and the oral production of a second language," **On TESOL '77,** eds., H. Brown, et. al. Washington, D.C.: TESOL, 226-40.

Homburg, T. and M. Spann. 1982. "ESL reading proficiency assessment: testing strategies," **On TESOL '81,** eds., M. Hines and W. Rutherford. Washington, D.C.: TESOL, 25-33.

Hosenfeld, C., V. Arnold, J. Kirchofer, J. Leciura and L. Wilson. 1981. "Second language reading: a curricular sequence for teaching reading strategies," *Foreign Language Annals* 14: 415-22.

Houck, N., J. Robertson and S. Krashen. 1978. "On the domain of the conscious grammar," *TESOL Quarterly* 12: 335-39.

Jordens, P. and E. Kellerman. 1978. "Investigation into the strategy of transfer in second language learning," Paper presented at the AILA Conference, Montreal, Canada.

Kayfetz-Fuller, J. 1978. *An Investigation of Natural and Monitored Morpheme Difficulty Orders by Non-native Adult Students of English.* Ph.D. Dissertation, Florida State University.

Kellerman, E. 1978. "Giving learners a break: native language intuitions as a source of prediction about transferability," *Working Papers on Bilingualism* 15: 59-92.

Kessler, C. and I. Idar. 1977. "The acquisition of English syntactic structures by a Vietnamese child," Paper presented at the Los Angeles Second Language Acquisition Forum, Los Angeles, California: The University of California at Los Angeles.

Klima, E. and U. Bellugi. 1966. "Syntactic regularities in the speech of children," **Psycholinguistic Papers,** eds., J. Lyons and R. Wales. Edinburgh University Press; 183-208.

Krashen, S. 1975. "A model of adult second language performance," Paper presented at the Winter Meeting of the LSA, San Francisco, California.

_____ . 1980. "The theoretical and practical relevance of simple codes in second language acquisition," **Research in Second Language Acquisition,** eds., R. Scarcella and

S. Krashen. Rowley, Massachusetts: Newbury House, 7-18.

_____ . 1981. **Second Language Acquisition and Second Language Learning.** Oxford: Pergamon Press.

_____ . 1982a. **Principles and Practice in Second Language Acquisition.** New York: Pergamon Press.

_____ . 1982b. "The case for narrow reading," *TESOL Newsletter* 12: 23.

_____ . forthcoming. "The role of input (reading) and instruction in developing writing ability."

_____ , J. Butler, R. Birnbaum, and J. Robertson. 1978. "Two studies in language acquisition and language learning," *ITL: Review of Applied Linguistics* 39-40: 73-92.

_____ , N. Houck, P. Giunchi, S. Bode, R. Birnbaum, and J. Strei. 1977. "Difficulty order for grammatical morphemes for adult second language performers using free speech," *TESOL Quarterly* 11: 338-41.

_____ , M. Long, and R. Scarcella. 1979. "Age, rate and eventual attainment in second language acquisition," *TESOL Quarterly* 13: 573-82.

_____ , and Scarcella, R. 1978. "On routines and patterns in language acquisition and performance," *Language Learning* 28: 283-300.

_____ , V. Sferlazza, L. Feldman, and A. Fathman. 1976. "Adult performance on the SLOPE test: more evidence for a natural sequence in adult second language acquisition," *Language Learning* 26: 145-51.

Lawler, J. and L. Selinker. 1971. "On paradoxes, rules and research in second language learning," *Language Learning* 21: 27-43.

Lester, M. 1970. **Readings in Applied Transformational Grammar.** New York: Holt, Rinehart and Winston.

Lord, C. 1974. "Variations in the pattern of acquisition of negation," Paper presented at the Child Language Research Forum, Stanford University, Palo Alto, California.

Long, M. 1977. "Teacher feedback on learner error: mapping cognitions," **On TESOL '77,** eds., H. Brown, et. al. Washington, D.C. TESOL, 278-94.

_____ . 1981. "Questions in foreigner talk discourse," *Language Learning* 31: 135-57.

Lozanov, G. 1979. **Suggestology and Outlines of Suggestopedia.** New York: Gordon and Brech Science Publishers.

Lugton, R. and J. Heinle. 1971, eds. **Toward a Cognitive Approach to Second Language Acquisition.** Philadelphia: The Center for Curriculum Development.

Lukmani, Y. 1972. "Motivation to learn and language proficiency," *Language Learning* 22 (no. 2): 261-73.

Makino, T. 1980. **Acquisition Order of English Morphemes by Japanese Adolescents.** Tokyo: Shinozaki Press.

Mallison, V. 1957. **Teaching a Modern Language.** London: Heinemann.

McClain, W. 1945. "Twenty-fifth anniversary of the Cleveland Plan," *French Review* 18: 197-201.

Meras, E. 1954. **A Language Teacher's Guide.** New York: Harper and Brothers.

Morsbach, G. 1981. "Cross-cultural comparison of second language learning: the development of English structures by Japanese and German children," *TESOL Quarterly* 15: 183-88.

Moskowitz, G. 1978. **Caring and Sharing in the Foreign Language Class.** Rowley, Massachusetts: Newbury House.

Neufeld, G. 1979. "Toward a theory of language learning ability," *Language Learning* 29: 227-41.

Newmark, L. 1971. "A minimal language-teaching program," **The Psychology of Second Language Learning,** eds., P. Pimsleur and T. Quinn. Cambridge: University Press, 11-18.

Newport, E., H. Gleitman and L. Gleitman. 1977. "Mother, I'd rather do it myself: some effects and non-effects of maternal speech style," **Talking to Children,** eds. C. Snow and C. Ferguson. New York: Cambridge University Press, 109-49.

Oliva, P. 1969. **The Teaching of Foreign Languages.** Englewood Cliffs, New Jersey: Prentice-Hall.

Oller, J. 1979. **Language Tests at School.** London: Longman.

_____ . "Language testing research, 1979-1980," **Annual Review of Applied Linguistics,** ed., R. Kaplan, Rowley, Massachusetts: Newbury House.

_____ , L. Baca, and A. Vigil. 1977. "Attitudes and attained proficiency in ESL: a sociolinguistic study of Mexican-Americans in the Southwest," *TESOL Quarterly* 11: 173-83.

Olsen, Judy E. Winn-Bell. 1977. **Communication-Starters.** San Francisco, California: Alemany Press.

Ommagio, A. 1979. "Pictures and second language comprehension: Do they help?", *Foreign Language Annals* 12: 107-16.

Oyama, S. 1976. "A sensitive period for the acquisition of a non-native phonological system," *Journal of Psycholinguistic Research* 5: 261-85.

Palmer, H. 1917. **The Scientific Study and Teaching of Languages.** Yonkers, New York: World.

_____ . 1921. **The Principles of Language Study.** Yonkers, New York: World.

Peters, A. 1977. "Language learning strategies: Does the whole equal the sum of the parts?" *Language* 53: 560-73.

Pimsleur, P. 1966. "Testing foreign language learning. **Trends in Language Teaching.** ed. A. Valdman, New York: McGraw-Hill, 175-214.

Purcell, E. and R. Suter. 1980. "Predictors of pronunciation accuracy: reexamination," *Language Learning* 30: 271-287.

Romijn, E. and C. Seely. 1979. **Live Action English.** San Francisco, California: Alemany Press.

Sampson, M., W. Valmont, and R. Van Allen. 1982. "The effects of instructional cloze on the comprehension, vocabulary, and divergent production of third-grade students," *Reading Research Quarterly* 17: 389-99.

Savignon, S. 1972. **Communicative Competence: An Experiment in Foreign Language Teaching.** Philadelphia, Pennsylvania: The Center for Curriculum Development.

Schlesinger, I. 1968. **Sentence Structure and the Reading Process.** The Hague: Mouton.

Scarcella, R. and C. Higa. 1982. "Input and age differences in second language acquisition," **Child-adult Differences in Second Language Acquisition,** eds., S. Krashen, R. Scarcella and M. Long. Rowley, Massachusetts: Newbury House, 175-201.

Schumann, J. 1978. "The acquisition of English negation by speakers of Spanish: a review of the literature," Paper presented at the colloquium on the Acquisition and Use of Spanish and English as First and Second Languages. TESOL Convention, Mexico City.

Segal, B. 1980. **Teaching English Through Action.** Brea, California: Prepublication Edition.

Seliger, H. 1975. "Inductive method and deductive method in language teaching: a reexamination," *IRAL* 13: 1-18.

_____ , S. Krashen, and P. Ladefoged. 1975. "Maturational constraints in the acquisition of second languages." *Language Sciences* 38: 20-2.

Smith, F. 1973. **Psycholinguistics and Reading.** New York: Holt, Rinehart and Winston.

Snow, C. and M. Hoefnagel-Hohle. 1978. "The critical period for language acquisition: evidence from second language learning," *Child Development* 49: 1114-28.

Sparkman, C. 1926. "Recent tendencies in modern language teaching," *Modern Languages Forum* 2: 7-11.

Stafford, C. and G. Covitt. 1978. "Monitor use in adult second language production," *ITL: Review of Applied Linguistics* 39-40: 103-125.

Spitzer, R. 1975. "Taking the pressure off," *Journal of Reading* 198-200.

Stevick, E. 1973. "Review of Curran 1972," *Language Learning* 23: 259-71.

——————— . 1976. **Memory, Meaning and Method.** Rowley, Massachusetts: Newbury House.

Terrell, T. "A Natural Approach to the Acquisition and Learning of a Language," *Modern Language Journal* 61: 325-36.

——————— . "The Natural Approach to Language Teaching: An Update," *Modern Language* 66: 121-131.

Thompson, M., et. al. 1957. **A-LM Spanish Levels I, II, III, IV.** New York: Harcourt, Brace and World.

Thorndike, R. 1973. **Reading Comprehension in Fifteen Countries.** New York: Wiley and Sons.

Titone, R. 1968. **Teaching Foreign Languages: An Historical Sketch.** Washington, D.C.: Georgetown University Press.

Ulijn, J. and G. Kemper. 1976. "The role of the first language in second language reading comprehension: some experimental evidence," *Proceedings of the Fourth International Congress of Applied Linguistics,* 1: 495-570, ed., G. Nickel. Stuttgart: Hochschul Verlag.

Wagner-Gough, J. and E. Hatch. 1975. "The importance of input data in second language acquisition studies," *Language Learning* 25: 297-308.

Williams, C. 1923. "¿Es posible pensar en una lengua extranjera?", *Hispania* 6: 102-5.

Williams, D. 1981. "Factors related to performance in reading English as a second language," *Language Learning* 31: 31-50.

Wilkins, D. 1976. **Notional Syllabuses.** London: Oxford University Press.

Wode, H. 1978. "Developmental sequences in naturalistic L2 acquisition," **Second Language Acquisition,** ed., E. Hatch. Rowley, Massachusetts: Newbury House, 101-17.

R. Yorkey, R Barrutia, A. Chamot, I. Rainey de Diaz, J. Gonzalez, J. Ney, W. Woolf 1978. **English for International Communication.** New York: American Book Co.

Zobl. H. 1980. "Developmental and transfer errors: their common bases and (possibly) differential effects on subsequent learning," *TESOL Quarterly,* 14: 469-79.

——————— . 1980. "Contact-induced language change, learner-language, and the potential of a modified CA," Paper presented at the Los Angeles Second Language Acquisition Research Forum, UCLA.

——————— . "The formal and developmental selectivity of L1 influence on L2 acquisition," *Language Learning* 30: 43-57.